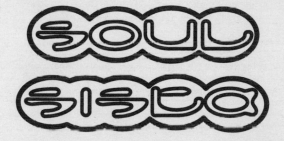

HOW TO BE A GIRL OF GOD!

BETH REDMAN

Hodder & Stoughton
LONDON SYDNEY AUCKLAND

First published in Great Britain in 2000

2

British Library Cataloguing in Publication Data
A record for this book is available from the British Library

ISBN 0 340 5677 2

Typeset by Avon Dataset Ltd, Bidford-on-Avon, Warks

Printed and bound in Great Britain by
Clays Ltd, St Ives plc

Hodder and Stoughton
A Division of Hodder Headline Ltd
338 Euston Road
London NW1 3BH

To Andy Hawthorne, for his input and inspiration,
and to Sophie, Loretta, Colette and Claire,
for the most amazing house-sharing experience ever.
Thank you for your friendship, your faithfulness
and your godliness.

Contents

Foreword

Soul Sista is the second in our Soul Survivor series
of books aimed to encourage, inform and equip
young Christians today. Beth Redman has been
part of the Soul Survivor team for three years
now. Before that she was part of the World Wide
Message Tribe, and prior to that she was a
member of Youth for Christ's evangelistic band
'TVB'.

The first time I ever met Beth I found her

'unusual', an opinion I have not seen fit to change as she has become one of my closest friends. Beth is unusual because she combines an incredible passion for God with an ability to do the unexpected, which keeps life interesting for the rest of us . . .

This book is Beth at her best on all subjects that are relevant to today's young women. As a man I read it with keen interest and at times wanted to shout, 'Eureka, so that's why they behave like that!' *Soul Sista* is packed full of direct teaching written in a direct way. Beth faces all the thorny issues and gives brilliant teaching which is thoroughly biblical, incredibly practical and also at times hysterically funny! There were times when I had to put *Soul Sista* down I was laughing so hard. Unfortunately nearly all the illustrations are true. We have a little rule at Soul Survivor that if something outrageous is going to happen, it will happen to Beth!

Most of all, this is an incredibly real book. Beth tells it as it is and is at times amazingly vulnerable. Beth is not writing out of some ivory tower. Many of the issues she deals with she has had to work through herself. I have been humbled as I have seen Beth face and deal with many difficult issues bravely, honestly and with determination. She is one of the people most open to the God of change that I know. As a result this book is a book of hope. God can and does change us!

Soul Sista is going to change many lives. Let is change yours.

Mike Pilavachi
June 2000

Acknowledgements

I would like to thank first of all my husband, Matt, for all his support throughout this project. Matt is an amazing listener and also a very patient friend – he spent many late nights helping me put this book together and I couldn't have done it without him. What a man!

Special thanks to Mike Pilavachi who has helped to make this book possible – thank you, Mike, for all your support, all your advice and for being such a brilliant pastor and friend; I love you lots. Thanks to Dawn Reynolds for her vision and for running with it so brilliantly. Thanks also to David Moloney of Hodder who has put up with a lot and has been a pleasure to work with. Finally, to all my friends at Soul Survivor Watford, especially Anna, who have helped me to have the confidence to do this, thank you guys.

Before you start...

My name is Beth Redman and I want to explain to you a bit about why I have written this book. It's because God has done so much in my life and has given me a passion to encourage young women like yourselves to go for it with him, to believe in his promises, to hold your heads up high and to 'run the race marked out for you'.

There is a guy called Winkie Pratney who called young people like you and me a 'survivor generation'.

We thought of this when we named Soul Survivor, and recognised that it is hard enough to just survive in these days. Times are tough and we need God.

A little bit about me: since the age of eighteen I have been involved with evangelism and speaking and teaching. I joined Youth for Christ's year project TVB – a band that travels the country doing schools work – and from there went on to join the World Wide Message Tribe in Manchester. This was a life-changing experience for me. I learnt to trust God and saw him work in the most faith-building, amazing ways. From there I moved to Soul Survivor and not only married my husband Matt but got stuck into training and discipling young people as an evangelist and schools worker.

I hope that this book becomes an encouragement and an inspiration in your walk with God. I have tried to write each part from my own experiences. I am not someone who has had an easy life or who has learnt the easy way – I've made loads of mistakes – but I hope that these experiences will help you to understand that God is real, forgiving and life-changing. Happy reading, and God bless you as you seek to live this life for him.

1
Bums and cums

You walk into a packed-out Miss Selfridge changing room and you take a look around. Your head starts to swim as you see pretty faces, skinny bodies all trying on the same size 10 mini that's now stuck to your hand with sweat. Heads turn and you feel your cheeks burning. There is nowhere to hide. Right here, right now, you have to strip down to the baby-pink, babyish knick-knocks your nan got you two Christmases ago.

Does that sound like something that has ever happened to you? Well, it's the story of my life! I am forever ending up in communal changing room disasters. Like the time when I was desperate to get one of those 'dresses to impress'. I sneaked in and was greeted by a whole group of girlies a quarter of my size. Pressure!

I undressed in record time, slipped the thing over my head – and that's where it decided to stay! I couldn't get it up and it wasn't coming down. I'm there in my non-matching knickers and bra with my 'badly needing a wax' bikini line, feeling like a rhino. I wanted to die.

Those experiences leave you vowing you'll never eat, shop or breathe again.

But where does that kind of pressure come from? Why does it matter that I couldn't fit into a size 10?

I can't answer these questions any better than a writer called Steve Mawston, who said the following in his book *Who Do You Think You Are?* (Scripture Union, 1997).

We are constantly bombarded with messages from the media. Advertising alone is a multi-million pound business, and its sole aim is to entice the general public into buying particular products by whatever means necessary. Advertisers achieve their objective by splattering our screens with images of the ideal body. It doesn't matter what the product is – everything from chocolate bars to cars to washing machines includes perfect curves, complexions and cheekbones. The underlying message is 'If you buy this perfume, you too will have the allure of Kate Moss' or 'If you drive this car, women will fall at your feet'.

Unfortunately, advertising has a dangerous side effect. Normal people like us compare our bodies to the models we see in those adverts, the movies and the magazines and we think, 'I don't look like that!' The media screams at our subconscious, 'You're not good enough, you're ugly. You need to look like this.'

- Perhaps this is why 62 per cent of girls don't like their bodies; in the UK alone approximately 3.5 million girls are anorexic or bulimic and are most at risk of developing mental health problems.
- Maybe that explains why we all feel pressure when

we walk into a communal changing room: no one is telling us to celebrate our differences, or rather our uniqueness. In my cell group there happens to be a large percentage of either very tall or incredibly short girls. Us medium-height people are very much in the minority. Perhaps that's why one Sunday I found one of the girls in floods of tears. She was beside herself with worry that she didn't look like the others. Was she doomed to be different? But what's so wrong with different? In an age where scientists manage to clone sheep, let's not let the media, or anyone else for that matter, make sheep out of us by convincing us that we all need to be the same. We do not.

- Anita Roddick from The Body Shop says, 'The next generation will base who they are on what we tell them.'

- Did you know that by the time you are eighteen you will have had 25,000 positive things said to you (mostly before the age of three) and 225,000 negative things said to you? Well, no wonder you feel naff.

When I was growing up my dad's pet name for me was 'Fatty'. My brother fondly referred to me as 'The Slag' and to the boys at school I was known as 'The Dog'. My mum once sat me down to explain to me that I was not 'pretty': instead, I was 'attractive'. Ten years later my husband often says to me that I look pretty, and I say, 'No I don't, I look attractive.' The throwaway comments often said in jest attach themselves to us and convince us that we are what they say we are. I hope that as you read this book God takes the sledgehammer (or should I correctly say 'the sword'?) of truth and breaks through all the lies and pressures that bind you up.

Refreshing truth

- The average woman in the UK is a size 14.
- It's been said that if Barbie were a real woman, with her proportions she'd have to walk round on all fours.
- Most magazines airbrush their photos – which means the images you are fighting against are computer generated.
- Jesus Christ compares you to no one.

- You are unique: there never has been and there never will be another you.
- Remember 1 Samuel 16:7: 'Do not consider his appearance or his height . . . The Lord does not look at the things man looks at. Man looks at the outward appearance, but the Lord looks at the heart.'

Jesus is the only long-term solution. Losing a few pounds, going on a good shopping trip or scoring with a nice boy only dims the pain for a moment. I see so many girls who, when they are given a compliment, say, 'No, I'm fat, I look awful, my bum's too big.' Or women who eat only cucumber for fear they will put on a pound.

God wants to liberate you today.

I always used to think that if I could chop off my bum, have my thighs lipo-sucked and my ears pinned back, I'd be vaguely attractive. I lived in disappointment every time I looked in the mirror or read a glossy magazine or looked across the street at an ultra skinny babe. Life is not meant to be lived like that. God hasn't planned for you to be depressed and disappointed over what he has created. Your

Father in heaven compares you to no one. He doesn't say, 'If only I could take a bit from Hannah and a bit from Emily mixed with a bit of Dawn, everything would be perfect.' That's rubbish. God is satisfied – in fact he's delighted – with what he has made.

God loves you as you are

You're at Wembley Stadium squeezed in with 60,000 other Robbie Williams fans and in the middle of 'Angels' he changes the lyrics and starts singing your name. 'Beth's the girl, she's beautiful, she's funny, she's my angel . . .' – and on and on he sings.

You'd probably faint, but once you came to you'd lift your head and walk through the crowd with the confidence of a supermodel; you'd dare to do anything, nothing would hold you back – in front of 60,000 people your praises had just been sung. Well, stop imagining it and start believing it. Better than Robbie singing it, God's singing it. In Zephaniah 3:17 it says, 'The Lord your God is with you, he is mighty to save. *He will take great delight in you*, he will quiet you with his love, *he will rejoice over you with singing.*'

God the Father sings your praises today. Right

now he delights in you. One of the important things about being a 'Girl of God' is knowing who you are in God, being able to lift your head above what the magazines and the bullies say and look right into God's heart and hear him above the crowd. Why do you think Psalm 139 is in the Bible? Because God wants us to know that he made us wonderfully, that he knew us in the womb and that he has plans for us eternally, because he knows we need affirming.

Can we lift our eyes off our imperfections and ourselves and begin to look at Jesus and know the truth that sets us free?

Word up

This is what God thinks of *you*, based on the following Bible verses:

- 'I made you in my image and likeness . . . When I saw you I saw that you are good' Genesis 1:26, 31.
- 'I put you together inside your mother's body. You are awesomely and incredibly made' Psalm 139: 13–14.

- 'You are very dear to me, and I love you' Isaiah 43:4.
- 'You are valuable to me' Matthew 12:12.
- 'You are my child . . . and my friend' John 1:12; 15:15.
- 'You are in me and I am in you' John 14:20.
- 'I have chosen you, you do not belong to this world but to me' John 15:19.
- 'I have forgiven you and made you righteous and clean' Romans 5:1.
- 'You are free from guilt and condemnation' Romans 8:1.
- 'You are my child and I am your dad' Romans 8:15–16.
- 'I am on your side; I am for you' Romans 8:31.
- 'You are my work of art, individually created by me for a purpose' Ephesians 2:10.
- 'You are part of my chosen people, a group of royal priests, a holy nation, a special people who belong to God' 1 Peter 2:9.

You are worth Jesus.

2
Boys

Boys, fellas, lads – whatever you want to call them, they're a strange breed. Now don't get me wrong: I love them. I'm married to one, aren't I! But when it comes to the opposite sex they tend to have a slightly different approach to all things girlie.

For example, shopping! Why is it that most blokes hate it? My husband Matt just about tolerates it. That is until I utter the famous words 'Does my bum look big in this?' Then he's off! Not that girls

and boys should be exactly the same, but it would be interesting to know why we are so different.

In the hugely popular book *Men Are from Mars, Women Are from Venus* (John Gray, HarperCollins, 1992) we're told that men and women are supposed to be different – we were made that way. Yet we spend most of our time wishing men were more like us women while men dream women could be more like them. Perhaps the author is right, perhaps we have forgotten God made us different.

One of the major ways in which we are different is emotionally. Often men tend to pull away and silently think about what's bothering them, whereas women feel an instinctive need to talk about what's bothering them. Take your mum and dad, for example. If your dad is stressed he will most probably go quiet on you and brew silently. Your mum, however, is most likely to want to talk about it and get her feelings out in the open.

No wonder we react so differently – we were made to think differently.

And that's why sometimes when we like a bloke and they go silent on us it may not be as bad as we think!

I don't know about you, but when I was younger, boys were just annoying little fleas which, if I could have, I would have flicked off Planet Earth and lived happily without. But at the age of thirteen something unexplainable occurred and for some strange reason

(I think they call it hormones!) I suddenly couldn't live without them. It all started with our local paper boy, Dave. He was three years older than me and gorgeous. One minute I was interested in the paper being delivered, and the next I was stalking the deliverer of the paper. I would sit on my window sill, looking out, singing George Michael songs into my hairbrush hoping he'd notice me. I practically went mad!

Naturally I can be a bit loud, but whenever I have fallen in love I have tended to go over the top and act slightly out of character. Have you ever stood in the freezing rain in a boob tube trying to catch a lad's attention while he ignores you and plays footie with his mates? It's pure madness.

We need to make sure we involve God early on in all the decisions we make when it comes to blokes. At one point in my life, I remember after making some very bad choices I decided I would ask God who I should go out with. I fancied this boy in our youth group and every day I'd go into my secret prayer room (the toilet!) and ask God what I should do. There is a brilliant verse in the Bible in Revelation 3:7 that says 'What he opens no-one can shut, and what he shuts no-one can open.'

At the time I thought to myself, 'If this is true and God really doesn't mind me going out with this lad, then I don't have to flirt, stress or hope he'll notice me 'cause it will just happen. God will open the doors. Alternatively, if he does mind then I know he'll close the door.' I never ended up going out with that lad, or several of the others I 'asked' God about. I believe God is really bothered about every aspect of our lives, and that includes making the decision about who we go out with. But he doesn't interrupt or barge in: he'll wait for us to ask, and when we ask he answers.

A few years ago I went to stay with some old friends who had moved to America. Before I arrived they told me they had some exciting news to tell me, something they thought was from God. I arrived and was handed the exciting news. A book. Not just any old book but a compilation of stories from teenagers who had waved goodbye to dating. Right from the start I had two major factors going against me: one, I was a teenager and two, you've guessed it, I was dating! After two weeks lazing in a hammock swinging at 90 degrees I finished it. I was left feeling a bit confused and a bit guilty. Who is right? Am I in the wrong? I turned to my Bible.

In my Bible concordance there is nothing listed under the title 'boyfriend' or 'girlfriend', or in fact 'relationships', but that doesn't mean there's nothing there. God in his wisdom has given us the Bible for help and teaching, and there's so much wisdom and so many guidelines that there's help if we want it. Here are a few guidelines to follow:

- **Helper or distraction?**
  The dictionary describes a helper as someone who spurs you on and assists you. A distraction, on the other hand, is a person who may actually pull you down or take you away from the things that are important to you in life.

  A boyfriend needs to be someone who helps you on your way rather than diverting you from your path. Does your boyfriend (or the boy you want to go out with!) encourage you in your dreams or divert your attention away from them? I've known people who started off dreaming about evangelism and ended up out of the church because they started going out with a distraction rather than a helper.

  I love it that on a Sunday night, when I'd rather stay in and watch a video, my husband encourages me to get to church and meet with God.

  Choose a helper!

- **Pure like you**
  Standards are important. It is great to have high standards when choosing a man! But make sure you are living those standards: there is no point

praying for a holy joe who reads his Bible and gets to all the prayer meetings if you would rather read *Sugar* and are only around if you're on coffee duty. Be now what you desire for the future. If you want a man after God's heart then be a woman after God's heart.

- **Self-control v going with the flow**
When you do find your man and you start discovering his erogenous zones, *stop!* There's nothing better than a pure relationship – spiritually, mentally and physically. Keep your hands round each other's necks, because one thing can and usually does lead to another. I've been in relationships where we lost the plot and ended up more physical than a pair of sumo wrestlers. Keep yourself from temptation by resisting the urges, or keep away from the temptation altogether. Avoid spending time alone with the candles flickering listening to 'love's greatest hits'. Keep your bedroom door open, get the worship music on and definitely resist going with the flow! Self-control is a gift from God: seek it out and keep it pure.

When we've gone through a list like this honestly we can immediately answer the more obvious questions:

1 Is he a Christian?
2 Do you really like him?
3 Is he going to pull you down or spur you on?
4 Are you going to pull him down or spur him on?
5 Can you be yourself with him?

Sometimes you'll have to make a hard decision, but in the end you'll know you've made the right decision by honouring God.

If he's not a God man, don't make him your man!

Word up

Just by looking at a few simple verses in the Bible, we can see that God has provided the answers for why and why not; he knows what is best for us and what will make our life complete, not complicated. Trust him.

- 'Trust in the Lord with all your heart and lean not on your own understanding' Proverbs 3:5.

- 'Delight yourself in the Lord and he will give you the desires of your heart' Psalm 37:4.
- 'Do not be yoked together with unbelievers' 2 Corinthians 6:14.
- 'Don't become partners with those who reject God' 2 Corinthians 6:14 (*The Message*).
- 'Flee the evil desires of youth, and pursue righteousness, faith, love and peace' 2 Timothy 2:22.
- 'If any of you lacks wisdom, he should ask God, who gives generously to all without finding fault, and it will be given to him' James 1:5.
- 'The fruit of the Spirit is ... self-control' Galatians 5:22–3.
- 'Be self-controlled and alert' 1 Peter 5:8.

Be yourself!

Last, when it comes to the lads, be yourself. Don't try and look like your best mate and pretend you love all your sister's hobbies when really you're a complete opposite. Be you. Be what God's created you to be. If a guy doesn't like you for being you, sack him, he's not worth it. If he'd prefer the girl who totters around in high heels and you prefer chunky trainers, then let him have her.

I am loud – not always, but mostly. When I met my husband, because he was quiet and a bit boring(!) I presumed he'd fancy someone quiet and a bit boring, so I spent all my time with him trying not to speak or have a laugh. Eventually I gave up because I couldn't keep it up. When we got together I found out it was my wild side that attracted him, not my fake side. Guys will always see through a faker. You are a unique human being: don't be conned into thinking that isn't good enough – work on your inner beauty by all means (in fact, the Bible tells us to do that), but let your outer beauty and the real you *shine*.

Just to make you laugh I thought we should finish with a few comments from the lads, seeing as this chapter is about them. Check out their news and views:

Riley

Q *Describe your ideal girl*
A She would have to make me laugh but

also have the ability to have serious conversations with me. She would also be someone who will encourage me in life and in God and someone who I can encourage in those things too.

Q *Three most important qualities in a girl-friend?*
A (1) To make me laugh; (2) to be going for it with God; (3) to be great mates.

Q *Biggest turn on?*
A When a girl takes the mick out of me in a playful way!

Q *Biggest turn off?*
A Self-obsessed girls.

Q *What most catches your eye?*
A A certain style and individuality and some-one who looks quite womanly.

Q *Worst girl disaster?*
A The first time I kissed a girl I was eleven. Afterwards she threw up!

*** PARTING SHOT TO ALL SOUL SISTAS ***
A Don't look for a husband, look for someone you like who loves God, and see what happens.

Jon

Q *Describe your ideal girl.*
A Someone who has a heart for God and who is good fun and has a good sense of humour.

Q *Three most important qualities in a girl?*
A (1) A heart for God; (2) you fancy them; (3) integrity.

Q *Biggest turn on?*
A A beautiful smile.

Q *Biggest turn off?*
A Marmite breath! Seriously . . . and a girl who is desperate to get married. It scares the boys!

Q *Should girls make the first move?*
A Not always, but I like it when they do!

Q *Best place to find a date?*
A Church social things or Christian conferences can be a good place to meet people.

Q *How do you know if someone's right for you?*
A I think you know deep down in your heart, especially after spending time with them and getting to know them really well.

Q *Worst girl disaster?*
A When I was fourteen, there was a girl I would see every day while I waited for my bus. I sent her a rose on Valentine's day and arranged to meet her. I waited at the phone box for her and when she saw me, she laughed and walked off. How humiliating!

* PARTING SHOT TO ALL SOUL SISTAS *
A Enjoy being single.

Zac

Q *Describe your ideal girl.*
A Dark hair, short dark hair. Lovely dark eyes. Sporty. Nice set of teeth. Friendly, warm and devout.

Q *Three most important qualities in a girlfriend?*
A (1) Love for the Lord; (2) sense of humour; and (3) good teeth.

Q *Biggest turn on?*
A Haunting eyes.

Q *Biggest turn off?*
A Stubbornness.

Q *Most annoying girls' habit?*
A Time spent getting ready.

Q *Biggest misconception about blokes?*
A That we're all the same.

Q *How do you know when a girl's not being herself?*
A Nervous laughter or her nose starts growing.

* PARTING SHOT TO ALL SOUL SISTAS *
A 'Select wool and flax and work with eager hands.' Seriously, though: be of 'noble character'.

David

Q *Describe your ideal girl.*
A She would have to be a Christian who is going for it with God. I like girls who are funny or who are fun to be with. My ideal girl would also have to be kind, generous and funny.

Q *Three most important qualities in a girlfriend?*
A (1) Character; (2) relationship with God; (3) looks.

Q *Biggest turn on?*
A A girl who is a real laugh to be around.

Q *Biggest turn off?*
A Girls who just stare at you, don't say anything and then just giggle. Also when girls talk about their periods!

Q *Should girls make the first move?*
A I think that generally it is something that guys should do. It seems a lot more natural that way. But if a guy doesn't get his act together girls should just go for it!

Q *Would a flirt put you off?*
A I think a bit of flirting is healthy if you fancy the person, but if you don't then it is just messing around with people's emotions and that's a horrible thing to do to someone.

Q *Best place for a date?*
A If you are old enough the pub is always good; a public place where you can chat and get to know someone. The cinema is good, especially if conversation is a bit awkward at first.

Q *Worst girl disaster?*
A The worst is probably when I was going out with a girl and she called out my name, except by accident she called me her ex-boyfriend's name – in front of the whole youth group!

3
Friends

Ever heard that old saying, 'do unto others as you would have them do unto you'? I tried it myself when I was little: I told my mum that she could go out and play till as late as she wanted and that she could help herself to the contents of my piggy bank (all £3.18 of it). It didn't work.

A few years have passed now and I'm pretty sure that it does work. I've stopped thinking about being nice to someone as some kind of contract, only doing

things because of what I hope to get back. Instead, I'm nice to people because it's, well, nice. If ever I'm worried about whether I'm about to do the right thing by a friend, all I have to do is ask myself how I'd feel if it were done to me. That usually sorts it out.

But that all sounds a little bit simple, doesn't it? Often we think that friendship itself is something that doesn't need to be thought about, that doesn't need to be analysed and dissected. After all, it's such a natural thing, what's the point of prodding it about? The truth is, though, that friendship is anything but simple, and, more importantly, it can be the source of some of the biggest heartache imaginable. So let's dig in.

The best present

It's such a horrible thing to be lonely. For years I lived a long way from my church – and not just in terms of miles. It was a lovely middle-class place, and I lived on this massive council estate. My school was a long way from home, too, and I felt really isolated and alone. I didn't have anyone I could ring up, no one I could pop round and see for a chat. Loneliness felt like a killer, and I hated it.

But now it's different, so different that I almost can't believe it. When I get in from work and am feeling down or lonely there are so many people who I can call up or go and see. I can be myself with them, trust them and simply hang out. It's such a gift to find someone who you can sit in silence with and watch the telly. I think that when you've tasted loneliness you appreciate good friendship even more, and, after all, being involved in good relationships is what God intended for us.

I'm sure that God could quite happily have kept Adam amused himself, chatting with him and helping out in the garden. Instead he created Eve: his mate, his helper and partner, someone he could enjoy friendship with.

You are who you hang out with

Getting back to school has taught me loads. I've seen things that I'd totally forgotten about and have been reminded of just how raw school life can be. There's one girl who I've got to know who has shown me how true this is. She flits around like a butterfly, moving from person to person. If you're popular, she'll be at your elbow, making like the two of you are best friends. As soon as you start to be yesterday's news and your popularity points take a bit of a dip, she'll be off to pastures new, finding someone else to be best mates with. It's a shocking thing to see, but the really sad part is that it's not that surprising.

Before we start settling into this finger-pointing routine, we need to remind ourselves of a few home truths: we might not be using friends like Madame Butterfly, but how do we feel about hanging around with that person who nobody likes, the one who's always left out, the one who is really hard to get along with? We are who we hang around with, and most of us don't like sending out the wrong message.

Get out quick?

Good friendship is a wonderful thing, but let's not be stupid here: we're all bound to have people dump on us in some way. We all mess up, and it's only a matter of time before we're on the receiving end. What should we do then? Is it a sign for us to pack up and move on? Does it cut us free and allow us to walk away? Sistas, I'm sorry but it doesn't. Instead of getting on the first train out, aggro is our cue to turn up trumps and be a truly good friend.

It says in the Bible 'as iron sharpens iron so one man sharpens another', and as we get close to someone we really do rub against each other, helping to knock off the bad bits. Of course, that's a tough thing to go through – painful and all that – but it's worth hanging in there.

The guide

Joanne and Sarah have been friends for a couple of months, but for the last two weeks Sarah has been in a weird mood. Instead of chatting to Joanne, she's spent most of her free time alone, refusing to talk about how she's feeling. What should Joanne do?

1 First up, here's what she shouldn't do: run off and tell everyone else what a complete psycho Sarah's being.
2 Give her space. We all need it, especially when we're stressed. It's important to respect privacy as well as to trust that we all have our own ways of dealing with difficult stuff.
3 Pray.
4 If it keeps on going, try talking. The idea here wouldn't be for Joanne to go in there with a 'Hey, you've been ignoring me' attack. Instead, the plan is to let Sarah know that she's worried about her and to ask if she might want to talk about it,

maybe so that Joanne can do something to help. And the best time to do this? Perhaps not in the corridor two minutes before double maths.

But what about when it's their fault?

Of course, though, there are times when people stick the knife in good and proper. What do we do then? Well, it's pretty low on fun and revenge, but again the solution isn't found in running around and mouthing off to everyone in sight. Perhaps you need a bit of space – which is fine – but sooner or later you're going to have to take a brave step: you're going to have to be honest with them.

This can seem so unfair: they've made you feel bad and now you have to feel bad again by making yourself vulnerable and admitting that you've been hurt. Far more fun to kick back and go in twice as hard, but this is where most friendships fall down. It is vital that we swallow our pride and tell people exactly how we feel. Here are a few tips:

1 Be specific. Don't go with the 'you always' or 'you never' lines. Pick one thing they've done, give a

clear example and explain how and why you felt what you did when they said or did what they did.

2 If they're not willing to accept it, back off and give them some space. If, at the end of the day (and after you've been open and honest about your side of things), they still can't see what they've done wrong and don't apologise, maybe it's time to move on.

3 But if they do accept what you've said, you need to be gracious and let it be. No bringing it up at choice moments in the future, no cheap gags or gossip behind their backs. What's done is done, and if you've forgiven then it's up to you to keep it that way.

4 Just because they've wounded you this isn't your opportunity to wound them. Keep it brief, keep it real and move on.

Friends with non-believers

I hate it when I hear of young Christians who have been given grief for hanging out with non-Christians, I hate it when they've been told that God wants them 'set apart'. Yes, God does want us 'set apart', yes, he does want us to be different, but if we're all hanging out with other Christians all the time, then who will be able to see us to tell if we're any different?

We need to have those friendships – those good, natural friendships with laughter, tears and trust – not to score points in heaven, but because it's natural. Look at Jesus; he didn't get people to follow him by filling out a questionnaire or responding to a bumper sticker on the back of his donkey. He introduced himself the way all of us humans know best: by hanging out and establishing friendships.

So, of course, we have to be friends with people who believe differently to us – they're all people made by God who he loves – but how should we do it? You want to know how we should behave differently in order to have effective friendships with *non-believers*? You want the answer? Here it is then: nothing. We don't treat people who don't believe any differently to those who do. We just need to be ourselves – passionate, hurt, caring and respectful. Just do what comes naturally.

It can be hard, though, having a friend who isn't a Christian: you love and respect them and don't want to force your beliefs down their throats, but you also want them to get out of Christianity all that you've got. But respect is key: your friendship isn't conditional, and if they don't want to follow you that's fine. Be open with them, invite them along to stuff, maybe say how you feel, but in general let your integrity and consistency be the clearest message of your faith.

Word up

- 'The Lord would speak to Moses face to face, as a man speaks with his friend' Exodus 33:11.
- 'A gossip separates close friends' Proverbs 16:28.
- 'A friend loves at all times' Proverbs 17:17.
- 'There is a friend who sticks closer than a brother' Proverbs 18:24.
- 'Wounds from a friend can be trusted' Proverbs 27:6.
- 'Do not forsake your friend' Proverbs 27:10.
- 'Greater love has no one than this, that he lay down his life for his friends' John 15:13.
- Jesus says, 'I have called you friends' John 15:15.

4
Pure princess

Don't let anyone look down on you because you are young,
but set an example for the believers in speech, in life, in
love, in faith and in purity. (1 Timothy 4:12)

So many newspapers run scoops on MPs who have
been caught out, one minute speaking in the House
of Commons about family values and then being
caught red-handed with a string of extra-marital
affairs. It causes confusion, doesn't it?! These people

say one thing and they do another. How would it have been if Jesus had spoken about loving the poor but crossed over the street when he saw a beggar? Or if he had joined in stoning the prostitute when just before he had been speaking about mercy?

As Christians it is so important that the things we say match up with the things we do, and that we lead pure, holy lives that are pleasing to God and an example to others.

In Leviticus 11:44 God commands us 'Be holy, because I am holy'. But what exactly does that mean? The word 'holy' is not a word we use much these days. It basically means to be set apart. Later on in the same book, chapter 20 verse 7 tells us 'Consecrate yourselves and be holy'. In other words, another challenge (and the Bible's full of them) to dedicate ourselves to God and set our lives apart for him.

It is so important that once we have given our lives to God we set about seeking to be like him, to be holy, to be an example . . . to be a 'pure princess'.

Sometimes I think if I could spend all my life mixing only with other Christians I could be really holy! From the age of eighteen until last year I worked for Christian organisations. But before that I was at school and then college. I really believed in God but couldn't quite get the knack of being a Christian during the week! On a Sunday I would sing all the songs and really get into what was being said, but as soon as Monday came along I was living such a different life. Holiness and purity are a lifestyle, not a hobby, and that's what I just couldn't seem to grasp. The fact is, God has called us to be alongside people who don't know Jesus. We call this 'being in the world', but it doesn't mean we have to allow the world to be in us. As they say, it's not the ship in the sea that sinks the ship, it's the sea in the ship . . . if you get what I mean!

Last Christmas the company I work for were holding their annual Christmas bash. I'd been told several times how wild it would be, and just before the night about ten people came up to me asking me how drunk I was going to get! My first thought was I mustn't go – all that sin everywhere, how will I cope?! But then I thought, look at Jesus – he didn't avoid the sinful places, he lived in them and was a pure example of God the Father. I'm not called to stay at home, hiding behind the curtains, afraid of

what I might see. I'm called to be in the world and be Jesus.

So I went to that party and it was pretty wild, but God was with me. I drank my Coca-Cola (!) and danced like mad. By the end of the evening I had made some new friends, and the next time I saw those people, half of them asked me how I managed to have such a good time and not be off my face. How exciting!

Getting back to the verse at the top of this chapter, 1 Timothy 4:12 is an amazing challenge that has affected me loads. Sometimes I can over-emphasise the first bit and get a bit proud: 'Don't let anyone look down on you because you are young' – fantastic and so true, but useless without the second, and in my opinion, the most important bit: 'but set an example for all the believers in *speech*, in *life*, in *love*, in *faith* and in *purity*.'

But how do we practically do that? Let's look at each of these areas one by one and find out.

Speech

> The tongue is a small part of the body, but it makes great boasts. (James 3:5)

> With the tongue we praise our Lord and Father, and with it we curse men, who have been made in God's likeness. Out of the same mouth come praise and cursing. My brothers, this should not be. (James 3:9)

With our mouths we have unbelievable potential. It says in Proverbs that words can be healing. However, the temptation and the trend is to be negative and clever with our mouths. Television personalities make millions from making fun of others, cutting them down and slagging them off. Apparently it's funny. We need to be an example of purity with our mouths and stand against all of that.

At work or at school there's always going to be that one person people love to pull down and get at. The challenge is not to join in. In fact, even to do the opposite and speak out against it. Or, even better, encourage and build that person up every chance you get. Each Sunday afternoon my best friend used to come round and we'd sit on my bed slagging off the other members of the youth group. It was so easy and always started off the same way: 'Did you hear about so and so?!' 'Can I just share something with you?!' 'I need you to pray with me about someone!' We call it anything else but what it actually is – gossip.

Let's be pure princesses with our mouths. Lifting each other up, giving each other the benefit of the doubt and being the one who stands up and speaks out.

Life

The challenge is not to just speak out purity but to live it out. At college I got really passionate about evangelism. Every day I would bring in my red Gideon Bible and share a verse or two at an appropriate moment! I actually got people's attention, and although I caused a lot of controversy people really started to listen. That is, until I started to confuse them. A bit like the MPs at the start of this chapter, I would go on about certain things and passionately air my 'God views'. But at break time I would go to the common room and smoke and swear, and then I'd go back to the classroom for round two! At weekends I would join everyone at the nightclubs, and instead of being an example I would end up totally drunk and get off with people all over the place. Monday morning came again and I was back with my Gideon Bible. What an idiot!

The respect and the trust that I'd started to gain were now worth nothing. My words were meaningless because they weren't backed up by a lifestyle. Please don't be like I was. If we are going to say we're Christians, let's try to live like Christ lived.

Love

Jesus made such an effort to show his love to the world, through his everyday life and ultimately at the cross. He has passed on the responsibility to us, to show his love to others.

If you take the odd trip up to London (or most cities these days) you would have to be pretty heartless not to notice all the homeless people scattered about the streets and the tube stations.

Here's a fantastic opportunity for us to be an example of God's love in action. God has challenged me not to walk by and judge, but instead to reach out and love. Twenty pence and a smile can change someone's day; a chat and a cup of tea could make such a difference to a person who feels no one is bothered about them. Sometimes we spend our lives waiting for some massive green traffic light as a signal to do something big for God and end up missing out on all the opportunities that are under our noses every single day.

Faith

If we're going to be examples in our faith we need to stick closer than close to Jesus, 'the author and perfector of our faith'.

People often comment on how married couples (or boyfriends and girlfriends or even dogs and their owners) become more and more like each other. Well, no wonder – they hang around each other all the time, and so they end up becoming more like each other. Like when I first met Matt. I was horrified to find out he liked to go to the cinema on

his own – like a right old billy, no mates. Now, unbelievably, I have become like him in his boringness! I too occasionally go solo!

The way to be more like Jesus is to spend time with him. Walk in the light, hang out in the Bible and strengthen your faith by being with him, and the rest will flow.

When I lived in Manchester a few years ago, I shared a house with these four totally mad Girls of God. They spurred me on to spend time with him. I'd see what happened as a result of them spending time with God, and I wanted that too. That's what happens when we are an example in our faith – it's infectious. It grows and it spreads to others. Get together regularly with some friends who love God and it will make such a difference to your own walk with God. Go for it!

Purity

In the dictionary it sums purity up as being 'moral cleanness, innocence and freedom from pollution' – the stuff this chapter is all about.

An area we are all challenged with at some point is purity with the boys. It is such a giggle when you or your mate fancy someone, but how should we act around them? In 1 Timothy 5:2 the boys are told to 'treat . . . younger women as sisters, with absolute purity', – and if they are going to do that we girls need to be pure in our responses to them. This is where we need to watch the flirting! Flirting is usually our way of communicating that we like someone and we want them to notice us. The problem starts when we flirt with anything in trousers. It becomes slightly confusing for the poor lads, and it just makes the girl look terrible. Flirting devalues, and any respectable bloke runs a mile – it's not nice and it's not attractive!

There are other ways to show a bloke you are into him, like having a laugh with him, hanging out where he hangs out and – more difficult – by telling him!

Let's be fair to others and to ourselves – once lost, a reputation cannot be regained very easily. Let's be known for our purity!

Word up

- 'Make every effort to live in peace with all men and to be holy; without holiness no one will see the Lord' Hebrews 12:14.
- 'You are to be holy to me because I, the Lord, am holy' Leviticus 20:26.
- 'Therefore, I urge you . . . to offer your bodies as living sacrifices, holy and pleasing to God' Romans 12:1.

- 'God . . . has saved us and called us to a holy life' 2 Timothy 1:9.
- 'You ought to live holy and godly lives' 2 Peter 3:11.
- 'I urge you to live a life worthy of the calling you have received' Ephesians 4:1.

I want to finish with the words from a song called 'Pure like you'. I really hope that we have become stirred up to be different and can read this song as a prayer. God can help us to take the desire for purity and make it a reality that shines out in our lives. Let's go for it and be pure princesses who live more like Jesus every day.

Pure like you

I am yours
And you are mine,
Friend to me
For all of time.

And all I have now
I give to you;
And all I want now
Is to be pure,
Pure like you.

I'm not afraid
Of earthly things
For I am safe
With you, my King.

And all I have now
I give to you;
And all I want now
Is to be pure,
Pure like you.

5
Bible and prayer

I always used to have a problem with the Bible. I saw it as a kind of textbook, something hard and dusty, irrelevant to my own life. It felt as if I was going to be tested on it, that I needed to get down and cram the strange words and stories into my mind without really worrying whether they made sense. It all reminded me too much of school, and I didn't like it. So, I didn't read it much.

Then something changed. I'm a bit of a Brad Pitt

fan. Ever since *Thelma and Louise* I've been keen, and for a while just seeing his name on the poster was enough to make me buy a ticket and see the film, no matter what it was about.

All that changed when *Seven* came out. Typical me, I heard about this new film he was in, and dutifully went along to my local multiplex, tissues and chocolate at the ready.

I came out shocked. The film totally messed with my mind, and the friend I went with felt exactly the same. Instead of spending the film drooling, we spent it trying hard not to pass out with fear. I've never seen such a disturbing film.

Anyway, my mate and I got home and we were both in a state. We were freaking out and desperately needed something to help with the fear. We decided to pray and ask God to help. I picked up the Bible and – remembering that in Ephesians it talks about Scripture as being the sword of the Spirit – got ready to receive God's help. It was amazing; all these verses jumped out at me, dealing with the whole range of feelings that were running through my mind.

I was feeling guilty that I had gone to see the film without having checked it out first, and I read a verse about God seeing the heart and forgiving us. It was as if God was speaking directly to me. I read on and found another verse that talked about people being lukewarm in their faith. That was exactly how I felt, as if I'd been going through the motions for years. They kept on coming, and soon I was feeling so close to God it felt as if I could have touched him. It was an amazing experience and I'd never been through anything quite like it before.

Since then things have been different between the Bible and me. Instead of seeing it as dull and dusty I can now think of it as being alive and awake, ready to speak words of God directly into any situation I could take to him.

Why?

But why is it that I spent so many years thinking that the Bible wasn't much cop? Why am I not alone in feeling that? The thing is that, for many of us brought up in church, we can get into the habit of thinking of Sunday School as being pretty much like regular school. There can be plenty of learning and not much fun (or at least that's the way I remember it), and it can be all too easy to get turned right off the word of God.

So what is it, then?

Imagine being stuck in a strange town. You're lost, but you know the name of the street that you're heading for. What do you do? Look for a map (unless you're a bloke, in which case you're probably far more likely just to keep on being lost rather than get embarrassed by having to ask a stranger for help). And that is exactly what the Bible is for us: it's an A–Z of life, a guide to every single situation we could find ourselves in, helping us make good choices and keep focused on God himself.

So what happens when we read the Bible? What makes it so special? I'll tell you what: the book is God speaking to us. And God, like many of us, has plenty to say for himself. He's bursting to let you know what he thinks about you, to tell you how much he loves you and what you mean to him. He can't wait for us to figure out just what it means to be holy, to live a life that makes a difference. And as for his son, well, there's so much that we can find out about both God and ourselves by reading more about Jesus. The Bible is direct communication with God, and it's ready for us to pick up right now.

Way in

Like any map, though, you need to know where to look. Just starting at page 1 and reading right the way through probably won't be much good when you're going the wrong way round the North Circular in the rush hour. We need to get into the

Bible the right way, and I've always thought that the best places to start are either the first four books of the New Testament or one of Paul's letters like the book called Ephesians.

The first four books of the New Testament – called the Gospels – tell the story of Jesus's life here on earth. These are full of stories about the man himself and are key to everything that we believe. Ephesians was written later and is full of excellent advice for life. There's so much good stuff in the Bible, but it can be easy to get bogged down by passages that take a little more hard work than others.

How?

Reading the Bible is important, we've got that sussed, but it's also one of those things that many of us find difficult. Life is so busy for us that it can be all too easy for getting into the book to slip down the list of our priorities. In all of life we seem to be told to do things *now*, to buy what we want when we want, to live life to the max and be part of something big. Doesn't leave much time for chilling with God, does it? We need him, though, more than we could ever imagine. This is the truth, and we need to sort it out.

One way I find helpful is to read it every day, in the morning before I leave for work. I like to think of it as my spiritual breakfast, setting me up for the day and making sure I've got something to feed on. Going without it can easily lead on to us losing our sense of excitement about God as well as our passion for living the life.

But let's be honest, it can be tough. I've been through plenty of stages where I've been well into reading the Bible, only to find that within a couple of months things have been turned upside down and I can't even remember where I last put the book. Eventually something happens and I'll dig it out, put a bit of effort in, and within days am wondering how it was that I ever let my discipline slip in the first place. Just because it gets tough doesn't mean that we should chuck it in; as my mother used to say, some things that are worth doing aren't fun. I know, it all sounds well boring, but it's true.

The Bible and . . .

Here's another secret I'm going to let you in on. Remember how we talked about the Bible being God's way of speaking to us? Well, it makes sense then that we ought to respond to it by speaking back to him. When it comes down to it, there's a partner that goes with the Bible better than strawberries go with cream, Ant goes with Dec or my husband goes with *Match of the Day*: it's prayer.

It's great to sit down with the Bible and ask God to show you whatever it is you're after. Say you're stressed about work at school: well, say to him, 'God, I'm stressed. Please show me something that will help.' Then read on, maybe looking at a bit from the Old Testament, a Psalm and a bit from the New Testament, and see what you find. Chew over what you've read and ask God to help you take it on board and make it a reality in your life.

But I know that when I get up in the morning I've got a hundred things rushing through my mind. God might be saying, 'Beth, I've got something amazing to say to you,' but I'm saying, 'Yeah, yeah, just let me decide what I'm going to wear.' Then I'm worrying about what shade of lipstick goes with it, and then I'm worrying about the shoes.

'But I've got something that's really going to help you today,' says God.

'Just a minute,' I say as I grab the remote and flick on *The Big Breakfast*, where usually there's some band I'm interested in. Then I'm out the door.

'Oh God,' I say as I sit in the traffic, 'please bless my day. Amen.'

Mmmmmm. Not good.

To be honest with you, this has been hardest since I've been working for a school. When I used to work for the church there always seemed to be prayer meetings to go along to during the day. At school, things are so raw that there's no chance of an easy ride. I've had to rely on God a whole lot more, but even then the prayer and Bible times can so easily get squeezed out.

What is prayer?

Let's not get all complex about this: prayer is simply talking to God. That means that as long as you're being real with yourself you cannot pray 'wrong prayers'. Because of this, prayer is not first about getting answers, it's about getting to know a person. And just as with any other person, there are different ways that you communicate. Sometimes we'll be going for a good old Deep And Meaningful, while at other times we'll be just chatting. There really are no rules to this thing, so try it out for yourself.

Jesus showed us something about it all in John 10:30. 'I and the Father are one,' he said. Throughout the Gospels we can see Jesus talking to his father, sharing with him, being one. He told us in John chapters 14–16 that we were one with him, too. He said that he won't leave us alone. That's nice, and for me it shows how we've already got a solid base for getting to know God; after all, if he's up for it then it's just up to us.

What's all this quiet time stuff?

As well as getting to know God and living for him, being a Christian often means getting to know strange bits of language and jargon. Take 'quiet time', for example. By the sound of it you'd think that it was best done asleep, but in fact it describes a bit of time set aside to chat with God, listen to what he has to say and generally chill with him. Nothing quiet about that in my book.

When you're in love you want to spend time with that person, right? When things aren't going so well, when you've been stressed and busy and you haven't had time together, what do you do? You hang out, chat and sort it out, yes? It's exactly the same with our relationship with God: it thrives on two-way communication.

Back in Manchester there was a girl I met who was completely aggressive. When we were first introduced I was convinced that she was a bloke, and as I got to know her over the week I was in her school I wondered what it was that had made her so hard. I also started to pray for her, asking God to break in and show her what she was really worth.

I prayed every morning and evening as well as whenever I saw her, and pretty soon I began to see results. She'd calmed down a bit, stopped kicking and swearing at us, and by the end of the week she became a Christian. It was amazing to see her transformed, and if ever I needed it, this was living proof that prayer worked.

Answers

'Ask and you will receive,' says the Bible, and it's great when it happens. Sometimes, though, the answers we're looking for don't seem to come. It can do our heads in; has God forgotten about us? Has he given up caring? Is he really there? We can go through all sorts of questions at these times, and it can often cause plenty of problems.

Take my husband Matt, for example. Right now he's ill. He's got a throat infection and he's supposed to be finishing an album. But he can't sing and he feels terrible. There are all sorts of things riding on the album being finished on time, and every night I pray that God will heal him. But he hasn't: Matt's still ill – in fact, he seems to be getting worse. So what should I do? Should I dump God and assume that he has forgotten all about us? That just doesn't seem right to me.

Here's the key: it's all about trust. Even though Matt's still ill I'm not going to give up on God. I'm still going to trust him, still going to believe that in the long run everything will work out for the best. I know that at some point I'll be able to look back and see the big picture, look back and see just how great God has been and how intricate and perfect his timing was.

It seems to me that there are three answers that we can get to our prayers: yes (immediately), yes (with a little wait) or no. If we're praying to God, believing that he really is as great as we claim, then we have to be happy and ready to accept any one of these replies. After all, it says in the Bible 'all things work together for good for those that love the Lord'. This is so right, especially as sometimes our idea of what is good is different to God's.

So then, Girls of God, we need to keep up with our relationship with God. They say that communication is the lifeblood of any good marriage, and I reckon the same can be said for a good relationship with God. Are we spending quality time telling him how we feel, pouring out our hearts to him? And, as communication is a two-way thing, what about what he has to say to us? Are we listening to him – panning for that God gold in the Bible, waiting to hear his voice in our quiet times? If we are, then things are bound to be on the up.

But there's one final catch. Communicating with

God isn't just another task like shaving your legs, something to be done only when things get uncomfortable. It's not a job to be completed and ticked off the list, allowing us to go out and play. Communicating with God is something we can always do more of. Don't let that put you off. Instead, get excited about it: God's got masses to say to you and as much time as you want to spend with you. Sounds to me like that could be the beginning of a beautiful friendship.

The girl of God quiet time quiz

I asked a few other Soul Sistas to tell us what happens in their quiet times with God. As you will see, there's more than one way of doing it:

Q: *How often do you have a quiet time?*
Michelle: Normally once or twice a day (sometimes none, sometimes twice!).
Susie: Every day if possible.
Jo: It varies: three to five times a week.
Claire: Once a day.

Q: *When do you have your quiet time?*
J: Either late or early afternoon, but never in the morning as I can't concentrate.
C: Whenever I can grab 30–40 minutes in the day. Rarely before I go to sleep or early mornings – those times are a nightmare.
M: Usually in the mornings, but occasionally in the afternoons.
S: Usually after breakfast so I'm at least half awake.

Q: *Why do you have quiet times?*

S: To commit the day to him and focus my thoughts. To bring him requests, prayers for others and have time to receive strength and love from him.

J: To spend quality time with the Lord, just him and me. He was on a mission, yet people's lives were better for meeting him.

C: Just to touch base with my father in heaven. To see if he wants to say anything and to make sure I'm right with him forgiveness-wise.

M: They are the foundation of my relationship with Jesus – without them I would have a weak and shallow relationship.

Q: *Where do you have them?*

C: Anywhere alone and quiet. Sometimes outside, sometimes not.

M: In my bedroom, or in the bath.

J: Anywhere quiet and alone. Usually in my room.

S: Mostly in my bedroom, but sometimes it's good to go outside and sit in a field.

Q: *What do you do in them?*
S: Read my Bible, meditate on Scripture. Pray for others and things that are on my mind. Try to worship a bit. Mainly it's crying out for more of the Lord and telling him how I feel about him.
J: Study the Bible, worship along to a tape and pray. But I enjoy just sitting and talking to the Lord the most.
M: I normally read the Bible, pray and read a chapter or two of a Christian book.
C: Worship, read his word, pray and shut up. But not all of those things, just what I feel is appropriate at the time.

Q: *Do you think that Christians have to have them?*
C: Yes.
M: I think that Christians have to have times alone with God without others around. It can lead to a lack of depth in their relationship if they don't.
S: Yes. It's time to quieten your heart and focus on God, putting aside the hectic things

of life. It's a place to draw closer to him and listen. I think it's vital: try living without breathing! We need his love and strength to walk the Christian life.

J: I'm not sure. They're definitely helpful – allowing me to draw near to God in a way that I can't do in a group.

Q: *Are they quiet?*

J: Most times, but not always.

M: Sometimes I'm not quiet, but everything is quiet around me – it stops distractions and helps me to hear the Lord.

C: Not always – often they are fairly low key, though. I feel that God really can be found in the 'still, small voice' (1 Kings 19).

S: No, not always. I often have background music on to help me focus. If I can I usually pray out loud or sing. At times they are quiet, though: listening, receiving or falling asleep.

6
Salt and pepper

OK, so we know that God has called us to make a difference in the world, to show and tell others about Christianity. The trouble is that we can get a weird picture of exactly what it means to tell people about Jesus. If you ask me, being an evangelist isn't just about being like those middle-aged men in shiny white suits who visit town once a year. It's not about getting up on stage with the mike and delivering a perfect appeal. Being an evangelist is not about an

event, and it's certainly not about shouting at people while you stand on the corner of the street outside Burger King. Being an evangelist is about your life, day in and day out. It's about living the life – just as Jesus did – and having the heart.

I can remember walking into town one day with a friend. We were chatting away about nothing much when we both heard it. We had been so absorbed in our own conversation that everything else going on in the background was just noise, but now there was one strand of noise that neither of us could ignore. It was the sound of someone angrily shouting. I could tell by the little bits of what I could understand that he was selling something, but I wasn't sure what. As we got closer we realised with horror that what this guy was selling was Jesus. As you can imagine, this didn't go down too well with either me or my mate and we both tucked our heads down, stared at the pavement and shuffled past as quickly as possible. In the minute that it took us to get out of Mr Mouthy's range we heard it all: that we were going to be punished, that we had turned our backs on God, that we were heading for an eternity of hell.

As we moved out of range we heard some others

talking about him. They too were angry – angry with him. 'How dare he say that to us?' one of them said. They all agreed that it was people like him who were the precise reason why they didn't go to church.

Now, I'm sure that our well noisy friend thought he was doing a pretty good job. He probably even thought that his actions guaranteed him a couple of spiritual gold stars as an evangelist, but to me it didn't quite seem to fit. How was all that anger, rudeness and aggression the good news? After all, isn't it the good news that we've been told to spread?

Why?

I've often wondered why it is that some Christians end up falling for all this Shouting On Street Corners stuff. Perhaps it's because we see the men in white suits do it so well, we see them deliver a full-on gospel message with all the trimmings and we see it get results. And what results they are: hundreds going forward and falling to their knees as they give their lives to Jesus. Perhaps this seems so irresistible to some that they can't help getting up in front of a crowd and having a go themselves.

I think it's funny too, because even though I'd rather be forced to watch endless repeats of Richard and Judy than stand up at the front of the bus and deliver a two-minute gospel message, I've got a feeling that things aren't quite as simple as they seem. You see, while it might be a bit of a mare for the time you're shouting at the front of the bus, once it's over, it's over. You can go home and forget about being nice, honest and vulnerable with people because, thanks to your two-minute gig in the bus, you've a juicy red tick in your Evangelism box for that year. What really takes guts is having the patience and the integrity to live your life where people can see you, and leaving them with a good taste in their mouth. That's what Jesus did, so it's good enough for me.

Salt and pepper

What I reckon we need to get hold of is this idea of being salt and pepper. As any good cook knows, food without salt is bland and unexciting. Wack a little of the old white stuff in and Bob's your uncle. Pepper, on the other hand, helps introduce a meal to the wonderful world of spice, a land where taste is technicolour and flavour is fat and feisty. We need to be salt and pepper too: salt in that we need to be different to the world around us, and pepper in that we need to help inject it with a good old dose of spice by following Jesus's advice on how to go about living in the world.

Finding the key

When I was younger someone had a word for me. They told me that I was going to be an evangelist. I was not happy. Being an evangelist was the last thing that I wanted; why couldn't I be something funky like a dancer or a preacher lady? The idea of having to regularly humiliate myself by getting up on a desk in front of my friends in the canteen was just too much to cope with. So I ignored the word and got on with my life.

It wasn't until a few months had passed that I realised how wrong I'd been. Suddenly I was hit right between the eyes with the way Jesus behaved in the Bible. It seemed to me that he wasn't into notching up as many people as possible; what he was really into was hanging out with people. Even when he was on his recruiting drive looking for disciples, he was gentle and genuine, always offering the chance of relationship, not telling them 'join me or else, scumbag'.

In Matthew 9:35 it describes the way Jesus went about his evangelism: 'Jesus went through all the towns and villages, teaching in their synagogues, preaching the good news of the kingdom and healing every disease and sickness.'

Can you see how he was doing those traditional things that we've grown to love – the teaching and the preaching – but he was also doing something practical: he was healing people, helping them, making their lives better simply by being around them, doing what came naturally.

Step one

The next verse makes things even clearer: 'When he saw the crowds, he had compassion on them, because they were harassed and helpless, like sheep without a shepherd.'

Jesus's reaction to people was simple: he had

compassion. It came direct from the heart. And so here we find ourselves at the first lesson to learn about evangelism: it has to start from the heart. It has to start with a genuine longing for people to come to know God, not a genuine longing for us to look good when we stand up at the front in church and mouth off about our conversion statistics.

Because we need to be filled with compassion before we get out there and try our hand at evangelism, it makes sense to figure out exactly where we can get our hands on that particular compassion. It doesn't come from straining, high fibre or a course in Hypnosis For Beginners. That compassion comes from one place and one place only: you guessed it, God. From hanging around with him and his son Jesus.

Step two

My old church used to regularly put on events at the local leisure centre. The deal was simple: we invited along all the non-Christians we could find, and the visiting speaker would shout convincingly for a couple of hours, at the end of which the nonnies would all trot up the front and become Christians. Don't get me wrong, seeing people become Christians is one of the best things in the world, but I sat there too many times with my non-Christian mates, all of us feeling embarrassed at the high-pressure selling that was going on before their eyes. To be honest with you, it all got a bit boring after a while.

There were other times when we'd take part in these evangelism missions. We'd get together and rehearse our drama routines as well as our little speech that we'd give to people when we knocked on their doors. Then we'd go out and do the stuff. At the end of the day we'd pack up, go home and forget all about it, switching out of Evangelism Mode.

It wasn't until I paid (yes, *paid*) to go to America to take part in an evangelism course that I figured out what Step Two was. I turned up at the training centre fully expecting to be given the magic formula, the winning words that would unlock the padlock and score me a huge rack of converts. So I was a bit disappointed when we spent the whole week doing nothing but washing cars and giving out free Cokes. It took me days to work out that instead of being a waste of time or a complete con to get money out of eighteen-year-old mugs from England like me, the course had got it sussed. Up until then all that I had been doing was telling people about stuff; it was just words, just a script. Where was the evidence that I was actually interested in people? Where was the evidence that I was putting a bit of myself into it, not just repeating something like a parrot? Where – and this is the key – was the passion? It's kind of simple really; if we like doing something, if we're passionate about it, then we're far more likely to give more of ourselves to it. We're far more likely to show signs of life and be more human.

Step three

The final thing we need is the boldness to go with it. When I was in WWMT I got left in school, in charge of running an RE lesson, with some of the toughest kids I'd ever seen. They were mainly lads, all puffa jackets and attitude, and I was scared. I remembered that in the team meeting that morning a letter had been read out. A woman had written in reminding us of Ezekiel 2:6–7: 'Do not be afraid of what they say or terrified by them, though they are a rebellious house. You must speak my words to them, whether they listen or fail to listen.'

Well, if any group were rebellious it was this lot, so I guessed that the verses were relevant. I felt totally encouraged and decided that if the Bible said that I *must* do it, then I would do it. So I did the lesson as normal, and then split them into small groups. I picked the group that was made up of the hardest-looking kids, and told myself that if I was going to do this I might as well go for it 100 per cent. I sat down with them and told them my testimony, explaining how and why I became a Christian. When I finished I put my head down – safely away from any eye contact and said, 'OK, thanks for listening.' Then I waited for them to start laughing, walk out or whatever. But one of them – the mouthiest one with the biggest puffa – spoke up.

'Oi!' he said.

Oh no, I thought.

'Say that bit again.'

'What bit?'

'That stuff at the end about the cross.'

I started to feel a bit more confident and told him

that I thought Jesus died for him, just as he died for me. His mates were shouting and mucking about and he told them to shut up and listen to what I was saying. They all listened, got excited and at the end of the week became Christians. I was amazed and totally encouraged. I found out then that if we have the boldness just to speak out, amazing things can happen. Without taking the risk, though, perhaps we'll never know what might have been.

But don't get me wrong, I'm not getting back to the man shouting outside Burger King; we've got to remember the context. If people are asking, then tell them, but don't force it down their throats or try to make them feel bad. I needed the boldness to carry out that RE lesson in the best way that I could. At other times we might need to have boldness to answer someone who asks us if we go to church or what we think about sex.

Word up

- 'How beautiful . . . are the feet of those who bring good news' Isaiah 52:7.
- 'I am not ashamed of the gospel' Romans 1:16.

- 'Preach the good news to all creation' Mark 16:15.
- 'How can they believe in the one of whom they have not heard? And how can they hear without someone preaching to them?' Romans 10:14.
- 'Your Father in heaven is not willing that any of these little ones should be lost' Matthew 18:14.
- 'For the Son of Man came to seek and to save what was lost' Luke 19:10.
- 'Clothe yourselves with compassion' Colossians 3:12.
- 'A man reaps what he sows' Galatians 6:7.
- 'Jesus said, "Feed my sheep"' John 21:17.
- 'Let your light shine before men' Matthew 5:16.

Results, results, results

When I was living in Manchester with the Girls of God we all got fired up about evangelism. We were really excited one day when two girls moved into the house across the street. As soon as they arrived we all went over there to lend them our kettle, offer them food and all that. I started going to step aerobics with one of them and the others all got involved doing other things with them. We were always round there, telling them about the stuff and inviting them along to all sorts of things.

The trouble was that they kept on saying 'no'. They were really friendly, but they just weren't interested in Christianity. We ended up getting a bit fed up with the situation, and I can remember feeling a bit annoyed with them. Then it hit us: these girls weren't a project, not a puzzle to be completed within six weeks or else. They didn't have a Convert By date on them. They were real people and they deserved to be treated that way.

It can be too easy for us to get carried away with the excitement of thinking about someone becoming a Christian, too easy that we forget what it's all about. Often it takes people years of knowing Christians and finding out about Jesus before they are ready to make a commitment. If we were a bit less stressed about getting the results and more focused on just being part of the team – sowing the seeds and waiting for God to do the rest – then maybe we'd find this whole evangelism thing a whole lot easier.

There's a lady I once worked with who was on the case 24/7. In her mind she was at work to evangelise as much as she could, and I had to admit that she

had a pretty well-developed technique: she had a booming Prophet of Doom-type voice, eyes that made you feel as though they were looking right into your soul and a wardrobe that hadn't been altered since 1983. Any opportunity she got she preached The Word, and more than once I found myself wanting to vanish into thin air.

I was sat having lunch with some mates from work when she came in and heard us talking. She walked up, stood by the table and waited for us to fall silent.

'Of course,' she proclaimed as she stared into my friends' eyes, 'you know why you get on with Beth, don't you?'

We waited for the answer.

'It's because . . .' we waited some more as she took a lungful of air, shut her eyes and said, '*she's got Jesus inside.*' Everyone looked confused and the lady kind of floated out of the canteen.

Being an evangelist isn't about delivering the killer line that will have people fall to their knees: it's about living a life in front of them so that they can make up their own minds. We're not there to argue, but our actions and attitudes should make Christianity without question the most attractive thing around.

One last thing. I've mentioned a few bad ways that I've seen evangelism done, but I'd like to end on a good one. There were a group of girls who became Christians at a school I was working in. They did so well, managing to go for it in their relationship with God at the same time as keeping up with their old friends and staying 'normal'. Each year the school put on a gig where pupils would get up and do their thing. This group of girls decided to do a song, and they did it to a backing track to one of the Tribe songs. They put together a totally funky dance routine and just left it at that. No preaching, no 'This Is A Christian Song', not even any fliers handed out with Three Steps To Becoming A Christian Right Now printed on them. Just a funky song and a load of passion. It went down a bomb, and for weeks people were wandering around the school singing the song. Let's leave people with a good taste in their mouths, leave them wanting more and wondering about Jesus.

So what are we saying? It's all kind of simple, really: just live the life. OK, so that might sound nice, but what does it mean? It's about being you, going deeper with God and allowing him time and space to work on your life. It's about having a lifestyle that matches up to the songs you sing in church. It's about having friends – not 'projects', 'targets' or 'prey' – and loving them as a great friend should. Finally, it's all about Jesus: what better role model do we have? He was honest with people, yet people crowded around him. He was on a mission, yet people's lives were better for meeting him. He was holy, yet the 'wrong people' loved hanging around him.

7
Bust the baggage

Today's television is packed full of make-over shows; make-over your mum, transform your house, re-invent your garden, lose weight in a week, change your wardrobe, improve your image – you name it, these programmes can transform almost anything. In twenty-four hours you see the dingy and the ugly made-over to become the bold and the beautiful. All you need is 'Handy Andy' and a few tools, and within minutes slick furniture appears from nowhere. It's all so instant and appears so easy. But unfortunately life's just not like that – transformations take time.

When I was growing up I lived on a council estate in the south, near London, with my mum and dad and my older brother. One of the earliest memories I have was of seeing my mum pass out because my dad was trying to strangle her.

When I was about five I went swimming with my brother, and people kept stopping us and asking why we had such terrible bruises on our bottoms. All I remember is wishing I was someone else. I made up a fantasy world. I'd tell lies like you've never heard before, to try and escape. I hated my life and I hated me.

When I was seventeen my dad was made to leave because things had got so bad. He moved away and I haven't seen much of him since. I was left in a complete mess.

Unfortunately my story is not unusual. There are so many of us who have been hurt, scarred or wounded at one time or another. Not everyone's story is exactly the same as mine, but so many people are carrying scars from the past. Sometimes we get up and we get on, but other times we find we can't

deal with things on our own. Without God we are left in a mess.

Thank goodness we're Christians. We know a God who can help us and heal us, a God who can transform us and take the awful things and make us new, as though they never were. He takes the baggage and the burdens and removes them. That's called healing. Ultimately it is only God who can heal us, and when he does it's a sign of his forgiveness and his amazing love and compassion. A make-over like no other.

In this chapter I want to finish my story and tell you how, over time, God has healed me. I also want to share with you other people's stories of how God has done the impossible, the amazing and the wonderful by healing them, too.

The next few pages tell the incredible stories of two of my close mates, Dawn and Taryn.

Dawn's story

I know a girl who hated who she was.

She covered it well. She smiled. She was loud. She was scared. She was lonely. She stayed in a bad relationship that caused her phat pain and messed her head up because she thought she wasn't worth enough to deserve something better. She was told she wasn't worth anything, and she believed it.

She longed to be someone else. She put dark towels over the bathroom mirror to avoid her own eyes. She cleaned everything with bleach so things weren't as dirty as she felt herself. She got into debt trying to buy her way out of unhappiness. She felt out of control. She felt depressed. She binged on food to feel better. She felt guilty so she starved herself. She had an eating disorder. Food was the enemy, not a friend.

She was ruled by thought patterns of

self-hate and hopelessness. She didn't want to be around any more. She couldn't cry. She couldn't pray. She was numb.

Then, just when she thought she couldn't take any more, God burst through her layers of pain and hardness. One day, she heard a song that said: 'More than oxygen, I need your love'. Through the song, she knew God was saying to her: 'You are my daughter. I'm your dad. I love you. I like you. I rejoice over you with singing. I accept you. You can totally find freedom in me. I am your hope in hopelessness. I am your destiny in despair.'

She cried for the first time in a long time. She became childlike. She sat on God's knee. She became vulnerable. She took a risk and jumped into God's arms. He caught her and gave her the power to talk to someone. A friend and a counsellor: him. He gave her the power to let him in. He gave her the guts to get on that journey of freedom, that process of healing. The guts not to give up. The power to kick the eating probs. The will to live again. Then he reminded her of a passage in *The Message* Bible: 'once in a tight place . . you gave me room'.

That girl is me. Dawnie Reynolds. Daughter of the King.

Taryn's story

I first became sick when I was two years old when I caught measles and couldn't recover. After tests I was diagnosed as having Nephrotic Syndrome – a serious kidney disease that went on to affect me for the next ten years. On more than one occasion my parents feared they would lose me, but God was always there and marvellously turned many critical situations around. Over the years my relapses became less frequent and I was finally discharged from hospital at the age of twelve. On my last visit my doctor called in some junior and student doctors to see me. He told them, 'Next time you see a little one very poorly, remember Taryn. She has been there, and look at her now!' There was no doubt in my mind that the Lord had healed me and I testified this to be true.

It was therefore a great shock when I relapsed at the age of fifteen. I was in the middle of taking my GCSEs and got totally stressed out, putting my body under immense pressure. I remember one Sunday afternoon it hit me that I could possibly be ill again. It was something that I had never thought about before as I had been well for so long. The next day I went to my GP, where I was told my old illness had recurred.

I remember feeling really numb at first, then really sick, then really scared. I hated being in hospital and spent only a week there. After a blood transfusion my doctors agreed to let me leave, providing I checked in every day, a good 45-minute drive each way. The months that followed were a very painful time for my family and me. I put on about four stone in weight and puffed up like a balloon. I felt like a complete freak. A lot of my friends gradually stopped visiting me, as I just looked so bad – I don't think they knew how to handle it. It was like I was in this big bubble and was separated more and more from the life I had known. I no longer cared about what I looked like, being bathed or even about my GCSEs. I had hit an all-time low. The only option I could see was suicide, but something was holding me back and I knew that was God.

I was so angry with him for allowing me to be ill again and to suffer so much physical and emotional pain that I tried to forget about him. But the Lord never forgot about me – slowly but surely he began to soften my heart and really challenge me. He showed me time and time again that if I only trusted in him he would never let me down. That wasn't to say that there wouldn't be hard times, but I had learnt that even in the most despairing hour he can turn things around for the better. As, through the skill of the doctors, he healed my body, he also healed my heart. I can now see all the good that came out of my illness. Not only has it brought my family much closer together, but it has also shaped me as a person and challenged my faith to take God's hand and walk with him even when there is pain or I don't understand what is going on. The tough times are when we need God the most. Faith is living with questions not always having an answer.

And here I am now, seven years on, fighting fit and feeling great!

All healing comes from God but can reach us in different ways.

Healing through worship

God's healing power can break through anywhere. God can surprise us and meet us in the strangest places. When we worship God, we come to bring him our love. It would be extremely strange if on my birthday, when everyone handed out my presents, I handed them each a present back. But in worship, although we come to give to God and God receives what we give, he is amazing because he also gives back to us when we don't expect it. I have been in meetings where I've been focusing on God, worshipping him, and suddenly I am in tears because he has started to heal me. Even as we are worshipping he is giving to us, healing us and speaking into our lives.

Healing through prayer

In the Bible it says, 'Ask and it shall be given to you, seek and you shall find.' Prayer is how we communicate to God the things that are on our hearts and how God communicates to us the things that are on his heart. As we pray we can open up to God – you don't need to be in a special meeting where someone invites you up for prayer, you can be on your own in your bedroom and God can heal you and help you.

Healing through counselling

Occasionally things are too big for us to cope with on our own, and we actually need people to talk to and to support us through big issues that we are struggling with. In many churches and youth groups there are specific people who are able to get alongside and pray and talk these things through with us. They can offer confidential counselling, listen to us and help us deal with the problem, with God. The word 'counselling' sometimes scares people off, perhaps because there are so many weird examples of it these days. But it's a good idea to get help if, like with my example, you feel a bit messed up and don't know where to turn. God can use others to help us be healed.

Healing through action

Sometimes we need to get up and do something. If someone has hurt us we need to actually forgive them so that we can be healed and set free. Forgiveness is a gift God freely chose to give to us. It's not enough to just know it – we have to live in it.

If I spent my life receiving but never giving I would be a pretty selfish, lonely person. As hard and as tough as it may be, as much as we have received God's forgiveness for us, we need to give his forgiveness away to others who have hurt us. Sometimes we need to act to get freed.

Word up

- 'The Lord is close to the broken-hearted and saves those who are crushed in spirit' Psalm 34:18.
- 'And by his wounds we are healed' Isaiah 53:5.
- 'But for you who revere my name, the sun of righteousness will rise with healing in its wings' Malachi 4:2.
- 'For I am the Lord, who heals you' Exodus 15:26.
- 'Praise the Lord, O my soul, and forget not all his benefits – who forgives all your sins and heals all your diseases, who redeems your life from the pit and crowns you with love and compassion' Psalm 103:2–4.
- 'He heals the broken-hearted and binds up their wounds' Psalm 147:3.

- 'You are the helper of the fatherless' Psalm 10:14.

At the age of eighteen I cried out to God. I simply couldn't deal with the pain any more. I had tried to live with it and had even tried to live without God. I was really at the end of myself. I stood at the back of the church and I started to cry and cry and cry, something I hadn't done for years. I let it all out to God. Every hurt I could think of, every argument, every blow, every one of my fears – they all went to Jesus. Up to this point I was so devastated about my past and all that had happened with my dad that I couldn't even sing the word 'Father' – which is quite tricky when you go to church! But there and then God revealed to me that the person I was crying to was my real dad, my perfect Father in heaven. I wasn't fatherless and I wasn't alone. I felt I had a dad again. My healing began. This crying went on for a few years. I'd go to most services, church weekends away and conferences and end up at the front crying and needing prayer. Although it seemed like a long process (and sometimes a bit embarrassing!) each time I got up I felt a little bit stronger, a little bit closer to God and a little bit like I could imagine myself getting over it at last.

I then started to meet up with some brilliant Christian people I could trust, and began not simply to cry it out with just me and God, but to talk and pray it out with others. This too took time: some things I was just not ready to talk about, but once I did I felt so free, as if they no longer had a hold over me any more.

I do not want to imagine where I would be now if God had not healed me and if I had refused to let it all go to God. I was so trapped by all that I had seen and by all that had happened to me, and was a worse person for it. The lies that I used to tell were a symptom of my pain and my past. I had got to a stage where I would lie about almost everything – it had got out of control and I was a compulsive liar. I was desperate to change and wanted to be able to tell the truth about normal things without fear. It was a hard and long process, but each time I got prayer, God helped me to tell one less lie. These days I can tell you the truth about me. I am not bound by lies and I am not scared of the consequenses of telling the truth. God has rescued me from something I thought I was destined to live with forever. I no longer hate myself or who I used to be. The feeling of being forgiven is amazing. And also I have been able to forgive my dad and start again.

Asking for prayer and opening up can sometimes feel like the hardest thing to do, but when it's God we're opening up to we know he will never leave us or turn us away. He will see our pain through with us, and in the Bible it actually says that he cries with us – because our pain is his pain. The liberty and the freedom that God's healing brings is like nothing else.

Usually in the world we patch things over or try to cover them up. In our spare room at home I decided I'd had enough of the 'elephants and clowns' kiddies' wallpaper. A friend and I set about papering over the old stuff with some lovely new paper from Laura Ashley. Unfortunately I didn't remove the original problem, and my lovely green flowers looked dodgy, bumpy and naff. I gave up halfway through and it ended up looking worse than when I started. God does not do a bodge job: he does the job properly and finishes what he starts – if we'll let him.

Talk all your joys and your sorrows through with God your Father. Be bold and ask for help – you will never be alone. God the healer and God the Father is the only one who can transform us and set us free. Let him heal you.

8
True Surrender

Ask me why *EastEnders* is better than *Coronation Street*, and I'll give you a thousand reasons. Ask me why Ricki is better than Oprah, and I'll give you another thousand. But ask me what good can ever come out of school sports days, and I'm a complete blank. Of course I know all that stuff about teamwork, camaraderie and fitness, but in my experience they were never anything other than pure torture.

One year I was told that I was running the 1,500 metres. I told them they were having a laugh. They told me that, yes, it would be funny but that, yes, I was still running. I was not happy. Fifteen hundred metres is a long way – even further back then, when I was a few inches shorter.

So the big day came and I'd done no training – well, no *athletic* training, at least. I had spent plenty of time in the days leading up to the race thinking about how important it was for me to do well; a clear victory could win me many friends and maybe, just maybe, a boyfriend. I was pumped and ready for action.

We lined up and went off with the gun. I went off

faster than most, giving it everything I had in some mad kind of sprint. I was out in front and feeling good.

After 500 metres I was still out in front, but not feeling so good. In fact, I was starting to feel a little bit ill. Within seconds my impressive lead had been eaten up by the other fitter, wiser runners, and after just a few seconds more, I was staring ahead, watching the pack get further and further away. I was stumbling along, barely walking, and by the time I was halfway, I was flat on my back, gasping for air and hoping that nobody had noticed.

Unfortunately they had – all 1,000 of them, plus parents – and the day went down as my most embarrassing moment ever. Instead of coming out with a gold medal and my pick of the boys, I left the field disqualified, winded and feeling more than a little bit stupid.

You'd think that after that experience I'd have a bit of a thing about races, that I'd avoid all mention of them. Well, in general I do, but there's one bit in the Bible that I still think is pure dynamite:

Therefore, since we are surrounded by such a

great cloud of witnesses, let us throw off everything that hinders and the sin that so easily entangles, and let us run with perseverance the race marked out for us. Let us fix our eyes on Jesus, the author and perfecter of our faith, who for the joy set before him endured the cross, scorning its shame, and sat down at the right hand of the throne of God. Consider him who endured such opposition from sinful men, so that you will not grow weary and lose heart. In your struggle against sin, you have not yet resisted to the point of shedding your blood.

Hebrews 12:1–4

I used to turn up at Christian conferences and festivals and soak up everything that was on offer. Every seminar, every meeting, every ministry time, I'd be there, down at the front, ready to get as much as I could out of it.

I'd get back home at the end of it all, full of resolutions and determination. I'd plan on reading the Bible in a year, praying for a couple of hours each day and generally spending most of my time in a wonderfully intimate conversation with God.

Sometimes my plans lasted a while – almost a couple of months on one occasion – but, in general, it would only take a few days before I got distracted and ended up putting God way back down on my list of priorities. I never completely lost interest, but all my plans of being a one-woman revival-starter who did nothing but pray, worship and pray some more always seemed to vanish pretty quickly.

Of course, I was behaving in just the same way as I had done with the 1,500 metre race. I'd get all keen but never be able to pace myself, all my good intentions only ever leading to burn-out. But unlike the race on Sports Day, this really mattered. This wasn't about being popular or looking good, it was about just how much my faith was a part of my life.

What kind of race?

You see, things changed when I figured something out. One day it suddenly dawned on me: Christianity isn't supposed to be like one long Christian festival, with thousands of like-minded people at your side drinking in the 24/7 worship, teaching and ministry. If that was the sort of race we were called to run, then it would be a total dream, the easiest race since Lynford Christie took on Beth Redman over 100 metres.

But life's not like that. It's hard. Really hard. It's the sort of race that needs to be approached with perseverance, the sort that needs exactly the kind of pep talk the writer of the book of Hebrews gave the church in chapter 12.

Fluffy trousers

Despite the fact that my attempts at the 1,500 metre race had been so disastrous, I was invited a year later to try out for a local running club, to be part of the sprint team. I was keen and, again, I had taken it easy on the physical preparation, choosing to hype myself up in other ways.

I've never been a big fan of cycling shorts, so on the morning of the trials I raided my brother's wardrobe, coming out with a pair of ultra-baggy tracky bums. The crotch was at my knees and the waist would only stay up if I tied a bit of string around it. Next up was my dad's wardrobe, where I found a chunky woolly jumper. I added to the

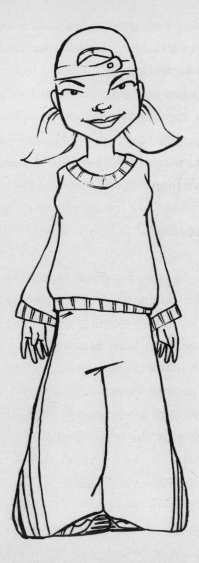

ensemble my own trainers (two sizes too small) as well as my Pizza Hut baseball cap. Backwards. In my mind I'd gone for the homeboy look, big style. I felt great and no one could tell me anything different.

I arrived at the club and met the coach. He asked me if I was ready to change. I told him I already was changed. He repeated his question and I repeated my answer. He smiled and escorted me to the track.

I did my couple of laps as warm-up, ignoring the fact that it was a deceptively warm spring day. It was going OK – apart from the few stares I seemed to be getting – but I still believed that I was a fashion winner.

Doubts crept into my mind as soon as the coach announced that we were off on a three-mile run. Oh dear. We set off and, like before, within a short time I was out of breath, out of my depth and out of time. I was waddling along, trying not to let my trousers fall down. I lasted 300 yards. I didn't get asked back.

Why?

Why did this always seem to happen to me? Why did I get all hyped up, only to end up flat on my face, humiliated and 100 per cent out of the race? I could cope with it happening to me on the running track, but somehow it seemed more depressing that it happened with my Christian life.

What I didn't know then was that – just like my baggy jumper and tracky bums – I was carrying the wrong stuff in my Christian life. Whether it was sin, hurts, wrong attitudes or beliefs, I was weighed down by all sorts of things that meant I was never going to be able to keep up my Christian good intentions for more than a couple of months.

Running three miles in all that rubbish? I was a fool – what was I thinking of? Are we in the same situation today, trying to go for it with God at the same time as ignoring the things that are wrong in our own lives?

Back to the Bible

Let's take it back to Hebrews. Remember that first line, the one about how we're surrounded by 'a great cloud of witnesses'? That means Noah, Moses, Abraham, David and God, too. What are they doing? *Screaming: 'Go on, my darling! You can do it!'* They've been there, they know how hard it can be, and they're longing for us to keep going, not to slip up and drop out of the race.

So, what's the prize?

You really want to know what the prize is? I'll tell you what it's not: it's not the chance to get up and preach from the platform. It's not the chance to dance with that funky band you're into. It's not pulling a fit boyfriend and it's not slimming down and looking like a star.

I'll tell you what it is: it's a place in heaven. It's unconditional love, eternal security and true intimacy with the creator of heaven and earth.

It's not a game of Snakes and Ladders, a game where if we fail we go back to the start. God's not like that; he's the sort who picks us up and tells us to keep going each time we slip.

Run your own race

Of course, it can be tempting to look over at a friend and try and get in on what they're doing. I've been tempted to do it with Matt, to coast behind instead of working out what God's doing specifically in me. Of course it's tempting – after all, it's easier to let someone else lead the way and take the risks. But the Christian race is about relationship, about getting closer to Jesus and allowing him time and space to work on and through our lives. That sort of thing can't be contracted out; we can't pay someone else to do our holy work. It's up to us.

No one can ever have your race. You're unique and so is your calling.

Pain and focus

But of course, if no one can have your calling and your race, so no one else will ever know your problems. Think long and hard and we can all come up with thousands of reasons why God cannot use us. There are the temptations we give in to when we're alone in our room, the attitudes we hold about the people around us. There are the hurts we've been through, the combination of shots that have damaged our foundations and challenged our security. Of course we've all got reasons why God shouldn't use us, even Paul knew that . . . 'Brothers, I do not consider myself yet to have taken hold of it. But one thing I do: Forgetting what is behind and straining towards what is ahead, I press on towards the goal to win the prize for which God has called me heavenwards in Christ Jesus' (Philippians 3:13–14).

Do you get the determination in there? Forgetting . . . straining . . . press on. Sure it's tough, but it's so worth the effort.

This race we're on has a great reward. It's also tough. So many of the obstacles that are in our way are put there by ourselves, whether that's sin or selfishness. Many things we struggle with have been put there by other people, the hurts and pains that we've been through. But still it's up to us to do it, up to us to pick ourselves up off the floor and try again.

Forget that person on your left or right, the one who seems to be having it so easy or who looks like they're best buddies with God. It's about you and your relationship with your Father in heaven. And how do we do it? We start slowly, pacing ourselves to go the distance. Don't try and be Mother Teresa by this time next week; try to be God's daughter, just that little bit more.

God has an amazing road for us to travel on. It might not be straight and have a smooth surface, but there's no one else who can ever run what's in front of you, no one else who can do what God has called you to do. God has plans for you, unique plans. Do you want to know something else? There is only one *you*. Run the race marked out for you. Be a fire-starter for the kingdom, fix your eyes on Jesus. Have you ever seen a greyhound race? Those funny-looking dogs chase after the toy bunny rabbit as if their entire life depended on it. Their focus is 100 per cent on getting as close to it as possible. That's the kind of determination we need.

9
Sista 2 Sista

I've done enough talking. No one person has all the answers, so I decided to ask a few other Sistas to tell us about their own lives and what their faith means to them.

Emma O.

Emma Owen is a dancer/singer with the World Wide Message Tribe. She is passionate about evangelism, about

*encouraging young women, and about her husband Tim
– who is also a member of the World Wide Message
Tribe.*

Q *When and how did you become a Girl of God?*
A I was brought up in a Christian home and I always
believed in God – but at the age of twelve I said to
God, 'I really want to know you personally.'

At the age of eighteen due to peer pressure and
boys, I turned my back on God for a year. Thank
God he didn't turn his back on me. With his help
and his forgiveness I put the past where it belonged
(in the past!) and I've never looked back.

'I stand firm in my ways, I give respect, I give the
praise' (taken from 'Girl of God' – WWMT song).

Q *Who has most inspired you as a Girl of God?*
A My gorgeous husband Tim Owen. He has
inspired me the most to be a Girl of God. Tim was
the first guy who respected me, adored me and
released me to be me. He saw my giftings and
qualities and encouraged me to use them to show
others that when we understand who we are,
daughters/Girls of God, and gain that security and

identity, we can be witnesses of how God intended our lives to be!

Q *Is flirting the best way to show a boy that you like him?*

A Factually, we are sexual people. We have been designed with hormones, but it's what we do with them that matters.

If flirting means showing someone that you are interested in building a relationship with them through chatting and smiling, I have no problem with that. If flirting means wearing fewer clothes, showing parts of your body, being provocative and a tease, then that's definitely wrong.

We need to be different to everyone else. God wants us to be pure, that's what should be attractive to boys.

Philippians 4:8 says: 'Whatever is true, whatever is noble, whatever is right, whatever is pure, whatever is lovely, whatever is admirable – if anything is excellent or praiseworthy – think about such things.'

God thinks you are awesome, beautiful and amazing. Believe him and don't degrade or devalue that which was designed to be holy.

Q *How can we keep it pure with the boys?*
A Having our feet stuck to the ground and never touching anything we haven't got is always a good place to start.

Today, society tells us to try everything, and that includes lots of sex with lots of people. But God knows better – after all, he did create us. In the Bible Titus tells us to say 'no to ungodliness and wordly passions, but instead to live self-controlled, upright, godly lives'. This isn't going to just happen – it takes work and the difficult word 'discipline'. Also there have to be limits and boundaries. Not only are we accountable to God, but it's good to be accountable to others, like a youth leader or a good mate. Finally we need to ask God to help us to keep it pure in our attitude and our actions.

Q *How does God help us when we mess up?*
A Daily I mess up – we all do. We do and say wrong things. The amazing thing is that there's nothing we can do that's too bad for us to receive God's forgiveness. When we say we're sorry he totally forgives us and it's over. Cos not only does he forgive us, he forgets about it. What we have to learn is to

forgive ourselves and ignore the lies of the enemy when he tries to dig up the past. God wants us to walk in his freedom, leave the past behind and move on.

Q *Most amazing thing God has shown you?*
A The most amazing thing God has shown me is that he loves me for me. He created me to be me, so what right have I got to change that?

I don't need to get drunk, sleep around or look a particular way in order to gain his approval. I already have it!

Q *What gets you up in the morning?*
A I am the worst for getting up, but once I am up I know whatever happens God is going to do something amazing. I won't always see it but I know it.

Q *Most comforting thought?*
A Nothing is going to happen in any one day that I can't get through with God!

Q *What's on your heart?*
A It's time to stop compromising. In the Bible, in James, it says, 'Don't merely listen to the word – do it.'

In life we are always trying to see how far we can push the boundaries away from God. It's time we changed our attitudes and started seeing what we can do to get closer to God. Being a Christian means being Christ-like. Is smoking, getting drunk, sex, etc., being Christ-like? And it's not just those big issues, it's all issues: lying, cheating, gossiping, stealing . . . we are all guilty of these – let's try and be Christ-like.

Q *Parting shot to all Soul Sistas?*
A To all you Soul Sistas out there, 'dream dreams' and allow God to help you live out those dreams. God can give you 'more than you can ask or imagine'. Don't limit yourself or God. Live life to the max!

Emily

Emily Layzell is married to worship leader Martyn Layzell and together they are assistant pastors at the

Soul Survivor Watford fellowship. Emily has the most infectious laugh you have ever heard!

Q *When and how did you become a Girl of God?*
A I became a Christian when I was fifteen. I come from a non-Christian family, and it was only when a team from the local Bible College came into my school that I really started to think seriously about what they were saying about actually having a relationship with Jesus. I went along to a service they were doing at a local church, and when the guy asked if anyone wanted to become a Christian I knew I did.

Q *Who has most inspired you as a Girl of God?*
A I think it would have to be two older ladies who taught me how to wait on God and hear his voice.

Q *How do we keep a good relationship with God?*
A Pray regularly, read your Bible and commit to a church. Also be honest with your friends about your relationship with God and listen to older and wiser Christians.

Q *What have been the highlights in your life so far?*
A Realising that God is real and that he knows me and loves me. And, of course, marrying my lovely husband Martyn.

Q *What do your parents think of you being an assistant pastor at Soul Survivor Watford?*
A They're happy if I'm happy. But I think they do worry about me spending so much time in church.

Q *How hard is it having non-Christian parents?*
A Very hard. Sometimes I would love to be able to offload on them about church and God, but they just don't understand. They think I am the religious one, the odd one out in the family!

Q *What spurs you on?*
A Remembering God's faithfulness in the past spurs me on for the future.

Q *Most comforting thought?*
A That God loves me even though he knows me.

Q *What's on your heart?*
A To encourage other Girls of God to pull out all the stops and go for it.

Q *Parting shot to all Soul Sistas?*
A Go deep with God, love others and be vibrant!

Dawn

Dawn Reynolds is the big visionary behind Soul Sista and is based at Soul Survivor in Watford. She is an amazing chick who has met God in an amazing way. Catch her story in chapter 7.

Q *When and how did you become a Girl of God?*
A Most normal chicks get into God because they need Jesus to rescue them – I became a Girl of God because I wanted to rescue Jesus!

When I was twelve, I went to a play about Jesus's life. Near the end, the audience became part of the play; they had this bit where some Roman soldiers were messing up this guy Jesus who wasn't decking them back. I got so upset – they were hurting this bloke who had done nothing but be cool to people.

I got out of my chair with fat tears in my ears and cried, 'Leave him alone!' My mate had to pull me down in my seat! At the end everyone was asked if they wanted to follow Jesus and live their life for him. I legged it to the front – I was gagging to save him but instead found out that *he* actually saved *me* from a messed-up life. Nice!

Q *Who has most inspired you as a Girl of God?*
A As a Girl of God I've been most inspired by my mum, who is the bestest biblical babe! She has shown me how to love and be loved, how to be real, faithful and gutsy in the toughest times. I've also been inspired by Steve Chalke, who has the guts, passion and heart of God to be a risk-taker, a dream-maker and to believe in me when no one else did.

Q *Who came up with the vision for Soul Sista 'The Event'?*
A The passion, vision and energy for Soul Sista came from a mix of things: from my personal journey with God – grabbing hold of his phat freedom that I found in the hardcore times in my life; from hanging out and chatting with loads of messed-up girls that I

met over several years through my work with Soul Survivor; and from chatting with a few buddies of mine who had a passion for girls – like Emma Owen from the Tribe, who said, 'Go girl!'

Q *How did it get started?*
A Soul Sista got started through sweat and tears, and with God on our side! Initially when I had the idea for a 'girl thing' I missed loads of sleep just thinking about it. I scribbled down my ideas and gave them to Soul Survivor, who I work for. We got way excited and got together a posse of chicks from different organisations to come hang at Soul Survivor in Watford for a day. We came up with the Soul Sista vision: a big Soul Sista event for teens and twenties, a mentoring forum – for young women in leadership and those being mentored – called 'Big Sista' and a retreat for young chick leaders called 'Sista Space'. The rest is history!

Q *What has been the hardest thing so far?*
A The hardest things so far are keeping going when it's tough, working through your own stresses while trying to help everyone else, taking criticism and

having a big faith in a big God when the money runs out – just to keep the dream alive!

Q *What has been the most exciting thing so far?*
A The most exciting thing so far has been to see loads of girls email, write and ring up saying how God has shown them, through Soul Sista, that they are 'all that' in him, that they have phat potential, that they are fire-starters – coming up with big dreams to rock mediocrity and injustice, finding that their identity and security is in Jesus, not image, and seeing that vibe kick off around the globe.

Q *What are the future plans for Soul Sista?*
A I want to have a crew of chicks working full time for Soul Sista, made up of dancers, singers, communicators, skateboardettes – whatever! I want to see them doing girlstuff in schools and at festivals, and being involved in community projects, taking the vision on the road around the United Kingdom and the globe.

Q *Most comforting thought*
A My most comforting thought is a phat duvet to

curl up in! No, seriously, my most comforting thought is that I am a daughter of the King, a princess, totally rocking with an unconditional love that is understated and underrated by God, who is my perfect Divine Dad.

Q *Most important quality for a leader?*
A I think the most important quality for a leader is character: a teachable head, a brokenness of heart, and a servant attitude. Oh yeah, and being able to laugh at yourself!

Q *Parting shot to all Soul Sistas?*
A 'Live to love and love to live.' Love God, love others, love yourself, love life.

Mary

Mary Pytches is an enthusiastic supporter of Soul Survivor. She spends her time being a wife, mother, grandmother, writer, speaker and trying to keep up with the '.com age'.

Q *How and when did you become a Girl of God?*
A I became a Christian when I was eighteen. Before that time I called myself an agnostic. I had never been taken to church as a child or gone to Sunday School, so I was pretty ignorant of Christian things. I began working in an office as a secretary and found the job utterly boring. I enjoyed a good social life, but nothing seemed to satisfy me and I began to wonder if this was all life had to offer. A friend invited me to a visitors' evening at her church, and because I had nothing better to do I went – fatal! I loved what I heard about Jesus and knew that he was the missing ingredient in my life.

Q *Who has most inspired you as a Christian?*
A Probably a man called John Wimber. The first time I heard him speak he spoke on the subject 'God wants his Church back'. It totally impacted me. Intellectually I had always believed that God controlled the Church. But when John spoke I knew that in fact people controlled the Church and that God rarely got much of a look in. The next time John spoke he said that Jesus only did and said what his Father told him to do and say. That was miles

away from the way I led my life, and I knew that most of the time I made my own plans and then asked God to bless them, instead of asking God to show me his plans and blessing what he was doing.

Q *Most amazing answer to prayer?*
A When I first became a Christian I wanted my friends to know Jesus. One friend that I had been at school with was living in London and I had very little contact with her, but I decided to get up early every morning and pray for her. It was sheer hard work – nothing 'blessed' about it. But at the end of six months, without me interfering, except to give her my testimony at the beginning, she became a Christian. I knew then what the great missionary to China, Hudson Taylor, discovered: that it is possible to move man, by God, through prayer alone.

Q *How can we be free from our past hurts?*
A Well, that's a very short question, but one which I have written about eight books trying to answer. I think there are three keys:

1 Forgiving those who have hurt us. Perhaps the most difficult, but the most important. For most of us this is not something we can do overnight. We work at it.

2 Inviting and receiving the healing power of Jesus's love. Only he can make up the deficits in our lives and heal the wounds.

3 We must ask forgiveness from God for the independent ways we have tried to meet our own needs, and in so doing often messed our lives up and hurt other people.

Q *What's the most amazing emotional healing you've ever seen?*

A A woman who suffered from claustrophobia (fear of enclosed spaces). When we prayed for her she felt as if she was in a small, enclosed space. I immediately presumed she was remembering a time when she was shut up in an air-raid shelter during the last war, sheltering from the bombs. But then she began to feel squeezed and pushed, and stuck all at the same time. It suddenly became apparent that she was reliving her birth. She was terrified and felt as if she was dying and would never come out. Eventually she felt a release, and we prayed the healing love of Jesus into her heart. The next week she came back for more prayer and told us that she had nearly not bothered to come, because the claustrophobia had completely disappeared.

Q *What is 'ministry in the power of the Holy Spirit'?*
A Jesus ministered in the power of the Holy Spirit. He quoted from the prophecy of Isaiah in his first sermon and said: 'The Spirit of the Lord is on me, because he has anointed me to preach good news to the poor. He has sent me to proclaim freedom for the prisoners and recovery of sight for the blind, to release the oppressed.'

What he did in those three years of ministry was through the power of the Holy Spirit, and he told his disciples that they too would be filled with the Holy Spirit and do the same things as he had done. Then on the day of Pentecost the Spirit came to the disciples and their lives were transformed. The Holy Spirit is the third person of the Trinity and is the one who has been sent to help us in our weakness to do the things of God. Without him we can do nothing. So any ministry must be done in the power of the

Spirit, otherwise it's human power and will not achieve the purposes of God.

Q *How does that help?*
A Well, it's the only way to do God's work God's way. The Bible says he helps us in our weakness. We are just frail human beings, and on our own cannot possibly do the things God has planned for us. So it's imperative that we get filled with God's Spirit and go on being filled with his Spirit.

Q *Most comforting thought?*
A In St Paul's letter to the Corinthians he tells them about his hardships, which are pretty terrible, but part way through his description his tone changes, as if he has remembered that for a Christian there is always another side to suffering: 'sorrowful, yet always rejoicing; poor, yet making many rich; having nothing, and yet possessing everything' (2 Corinthians 6:10). In my lifetime I have often been sorrowful, materially on the poor side, and sometimes possessing very little, but I have always felt comforted by St Paul's outlook on life. We may be sad, poor and have very little of this world's goodies,

but at the same time we can rejoice, we are rich and we do, in fact, possess everything worth possessing.

Q *What's on your heart?*
A I have many things on my heart. One of them is to see a Church in which my eleven grandchildren will feel at home. The message of the gospel never changes, the need to worship God never changes, but the way we present the gospel and the way in which we worship has to change to fit the culture. Sadly this is not happening in many places. It will be up to the younger generation to set this to rights. At the same time we 'wrinklies' can't just turn our backs: we must dig in our pockets to make this happen, or there won't be a Church of the future for our children or our children's children.

Q *Parting shot to all Soul Sistas?*
A No one may ever have affirmed you as a woman and told you what a special role you have to play in God's world. If they haven't, you may sometimes have doubts about yourself and your identity. Well, I would want to affirm the place of women in society today. You are a child of a Living God, a God who

has a purpose for each of his children. You may be a raging feminist – that's OK, but don't forget the old adage 'the hand that rocks the cradle rules the world'. It's a great calling to be a wife and mother, and we must never underestimate the power of a mother's influence on the next generation. Or you may be one of the Sistas who feels a little bit of a second-class citizen. And to you I'd say: 'Don't let past experience rob you of your potential. You are as special and precious to God as any man. Hold your head up; don't be afraid to be different. The world would be a poorer place without the input of us women! So get out there, find God's purpose for you and play your part in the world that God made.'

Colette

Colette Smethurst is twenty-three and a dancer and singer in the World Wide Message Tribe. She is married to Mark, who leads the Wythenshawe Eden project. She's also an amazing cook!

Q *When and how did you become a Girl of God?*
A Becoming a Girl of God has been a bit of a process

for me, rather than an overnight transformation. After being brought up by Christian parents, attending church from the age of two weeks(!), I did the usual thing and rebelled against the oldies! When I realised that actually the grass wasn't greener on the other side I came back to my roots and decided that God was worth another shot. I was eighteen years old then, and, as corny as it sounds, I haven't looked back since.

Q *Who has most inspired you as a Girl of God?*
A No big names really, just everyday ordinary women who've lived their lives in front of me and were an example of godliness (anyone can shout words off a stage . . . but these people really live it).

When I was eighteen, and at a really critical point in my life, I met a girl on holiday who told me and showed me about the reality of Jesus. Before that he'd just been some bloke in a book. Then I moved to Manchester into a house with three other girlies (one of them was Beth!) and we experienced the presence of God in the most amazing way . . . the reality thing that I'd always struggled with was taken to a new level. I now see my grandma and my mum as hugely inspirational women – but I never appreciated that back then!

Q *What is evangelism?*
A I heard a great quote from a guy called St Francis of Assisi: 'Preach Christ at all times, and when necessary use words' – I love that! Evangelism is so much more than words that someone speaks off a stage with a microphone . . . it's us getting out and living lives that show 'what Jesus would do' in our neighbourhoods, schools, colleges, workplaces, family, etc.

Q *Why is it so important?*
A Because it's at the centre of God's heart . . . in fact it was one of the few commands Jesus gave when he was on the earth. If I knew that a load of people were dying from some terrible disease and I had the cure, I'd be totally foolish and selfish not to let them in on it . . . how much more amazing is the news of Jesus?!

Q *Did you find it hard being a Christian at school?*
A I found it near on impossible . . . but then I didn't

do myself any favours either! I was massively insecure
back then, totally unsure of myself, my identity and
certainly God! As a result, I felt embarrassed by my
church and ashamed of anything to do with
Christianity. I was absolutely terrified when my
mum once came to school to give out Bibles with
the Gideons! And, without wanting to, I was giving
off the signal that Christianity was some huge
hereditary disease that I had no choice in, and that
people should avoid it at all costs!

Q *What advice would you give to someone who is
also finding it hard?*

A Be loud and be proud! That's not to say you need
to stand on your desk halfway through a lesson and
tell the class you've been 'washed in the blood of the
Lamb' (although, if that's your bag, baby . . .). Just
know that you don't have to make excuses for your
church or your beliefs, however politically incorrect
that may seem. It ain't a weakness – you're in a
friendship with the creator of the universe! How cool
is that?! I know it's easy to write on paper, and putting
it into practice is another matter, but I'm convinced
that if I could turn back the clocks knowing what I

now know about God (and myself) it would be a whole different ball game!

Q *Most amazing thing about being in the World Wide Message Tribe?*
A It's got to be the opportunities we get to tell people about Jesus, whether that's to a classroom of fourteen-year-olds, at a gig to thousands . . . or even, now and again, to millions of viewers through a TV programme . . . we just Bible-bash everyone we meet! It's nice for me to get a chance to be loud and proud, especially as at school I'd kept quiet for many years. But I realise, actually, that I'll never make the same impact a fellow schoolmate could.

Q *Most comforting thought?*
A Right now it's being on holiday! . . . with my husband, getting lots of sleep, eating lots of food, and generally putting my feet up!

Q *What's on your heart right now?*
A I'm part of the Eden project in Wythenshawe, so that community is heavily on my heart. What I really want to be is an intercessor – someone who

stands in the gap between a person and God and seeks to change the situation . . . I've not got there yet!

Q *Parting shot to all Soul Sistas?*
A It says in the Bible, in a book called James, that our lives are like a mist that appears for a little while and then vanishes. We get so hung up with this world and our lives here, and we forget how small and insignificant it is compared with eternity. You don't get a second chance – this isn't a dress rehearsal. Live your life in the light of eternity and seize every opportunity!

Anna

Anna Smith, aged twenty-five, has been married to Martin (of Delirious?) for six years, and they have two wonderful children – Elle-Anna Joyful (three, going on eighteen!) and Noah Jasper James (one year old and the spitting image of Martin!). They're expecting their third baby so life is busy and exciting. Anna loves to dance and feels really strongly about seeing others set free to do so. Arun Community

Church is a big part of her life and she loves the 'support and encouragement that we have there'.

Q *When and how did you become a Girl of God?*
A I was brought up in a Christian home with fantastic parents, which was a great help and influence. But I guess I made my own choices around seven to eight-ish, when even at a young age I knew God had spoken to me personally about following him.

Q *Who has most inspired you as a Girl of God?*
A First, my husband, Martin, has really encouraged me simply to be a 'God pleaser'. And the other person is my sister, Becca, who continually inspires me with a zeal for God like no one else I've met.

Q *How long have you been married?*
A Six fantastic years.

Q *How long did you go out before you were married, and what was that like?*
A We were going out for eighteen months before we were married, and we had a great time getting to

know each other. We both got married young, convinced we knew what we were doing, but it is only in recent years that we have really become each other's best friend and realised how great it is to be together and completely in love.

Q *Is it essential to be married to a Christian?*
A From my experience, yes. Believing in the same things will help any relationship long-term.

Q *Is sex worth waiting for?*
A Yeah, baby!

Q *Is it overrated?*
A Sometimes.

Q *Most comforting thought?*
A To know I'm completely in love and feel completely loved.

Q *What's on your heart right now?*
A I really feel that right now I want to be the best wife and mother I can possibly be and completely obedient to God in everything I do!

Q *Parting shot to all Soul Sistas?*
A Keep obedient to God in all you do, say and think, and you will live the most radical life you could dream of.

Emma B.

After an abortive attempt to become a doctor, Emma Borlase moved back to Watford feeling a bit confused. Thankfully, God was less confused and Emma gradually discovered a passion for listening to people. She also discovered Craig, and they got married in 1997. Emma now manages Signpost, a young people's counselling service in Watford, while Craig works from home as a freelance writer. They are both part of Soul Survivor Watford.

Q *When and how did you become a Girl of God?*
A I was seven when I 'officially' asked God into my life, although I had begun getting to know him from the beginning. When I was thirteen I got worried that perhaps he hadn't heard me the first time, and so I recommitted my life a further six times during the year, just to be on the safe side.

Gradually I've learnt that God listens much more closely than I thought he did when I was thirteen. He's taught me that he doesn't play games with his people, he loves them and longs to be alongside them. I would say that I was a Girl of God from the start of my life – but I'm certainly not the finished product yet.

Q *Who has most inspired you as a Christian?*
A I don't really have one or two people who I wholeheartedly try to emulate. I think I've gradually come to realise that we are all full of stuff that isn't sorted out yet, and there's only one person who really deserves to be put on a pedestal. However, lots of different people have inspired me in different ways, usually because of specific parts of their character that seem especially godly.

Q *Who is your best friend?*
A Craig.

Q *What makes a good friend?*
A The ability to let another person really be themselves. My closest friends have seen me at my

worst but still love me. They can be honest with me without making me feel bad, and they also trust me with important parts of their own lives. Good friends encourage, comfort and inspire me – and they know how to have fun.

Q *What makes a good boyfriend?*
A All of the above. I think it all starts with trusting the other person enough to communicate about the most vulnerable parts of yourself. If a boyfriend can do that, and you feel brave enough to do the same, then you've got the start of something good.

Q *Most comforting thoughts?*
A I am loved and chosen by God. He's done everything that needs to be done to restore our relationship, and I don't have to earn his love and approval.

The best things on earth are just a shadow of what's to come.

Cats always love you.

Q *Most amazing answer to prayer?*
A That my whole life really was turned around when

I prayed that God would come into it and make a difference. I feel as though every day I experience a bit more of the answer to the prayer that I prayed when I was seven.

Q *Best book in the Bible?*
A This question is too hard. I'll have to cheat and say the Gospels and the Psalms. The Psalms have always seemed to put words to my feelings and helped me express them honestly to God. Reading the Gospels is like being on a roller-coaster ride with the most radical, loving and awe-inspiring person who's ever walked on the earth. Realising at the same time that he was God's son, sent to change my eternity, is almost too mind-blowing to comprehend.

Q *What's on your heart?*
A I want to have integrity.

Q *Parting shot for all Soul Sistas?*
A Sometimes the 'vision' God has for your life is simply about living his way in a world that has a different set of rules. I wonder if we make it all too complicated sometimes, and we think we have to be

giants of faith with big plans and abilities. I think that the biggest act of faith is to live a quietly radical life – no trumpets, no autographs, but lots of small, difficult choices each day.

Before you finish...

So as you now come to close this book, I hope that God has spoken to you and inspired you. I started this book with a quote from a guy called Winkie Pratney who said that this is a 'survivor generation'. Your friends who don't know Jesus survive by clinging on to the world, but those of us who know Jesus survive by clinging on to him. A Christian life that's just church and knowledge is dull and boring, but a Christian faith that's real and living is life-changing and world-changing.

In this fickle world we live in, let's not forget all that God has done *for us*. In Psalm 103 it tells us, 'forget not all his benefits – who forgives all your sins and heals all your diseases, who redeems your life from the pit and crowns you with love and compassion, who satisfies your desires with good things so that your youth is renewed like the eagle's'.

Going back to the beginning of that verse it is so easy – in the midst of all the pressures and the struggles that we live with – to forget all 'his benefits', to forget that all our sins are forgiven. So often we live with the guilt and the shame of our pasts and we have this conflict with God – we keep reminding him when he has forgotten!

He has redeemed your life from the pit, and you're not in that pit any more. He crowns your life with love and compassion. In the school that I work in, you see all these young people and it's like they wear these labels: 'bitterness', 'poverty', 'lust', 'depression'. I used to walk round with 'self-hate' written all over me. But when we come to know Jesus he rubs all that out, and in its place he puts on our head a crown of love and compassion. That's on your head now; his great love is tattooed (not literally!) on your head and it will never be rubbed off. So lift up your head and know that you are loved.

Finally, it says that 'he satisfies your desires with good things'. When I first read that I couldn't believe it. We follow a God who not only loves us completely, forgives us entirely and rescues us, but also wants good things for us eternally. In Jeremiah 29:11 it says, ' "For I know the plans I have for you," declares the Lord, "plans to prosper you and not to harm you, plans to give you hope and a future." '

Just as you dream dreams for your life, God has dreams and plans for you too. Make your plans with him and trust and believe that he will 'satisfy your desires with good things'. He has not only done so much for us, but there is so much he can do through us. Don't just live this life for you. Live it for Jesus, let him use you at school, at work, at church, at home . . . wherever you go he can work through you to show others his amazing love. Realise your potential, not when you're an adult, but today . . . now . . . seize the day and live this life for him.

And never forget that God is always with us. He has promised never to leave us or forsake us. He is a friend when we feel lonely and afraid, he is a Father when we feel hurt and betrayed. We are never alone. God is walking through everything with us: our exams, our boyfriends, our mistakes, our successes. He's with us through it all.

So I pray that you Girls of God will be just that, and live passionate, radical and pure lives for him. Our lives are but a breath, it says in the Bible, and what that means is we are only here once – how are you going to choose to live? Choose God and live God-style! Know his truth, lift up your head and run with him.

'Abandon yourself as much as you can to God, until your last breath, and he will never forsake you' (François Fenelon).

God bless you on your journey, fellow Soul Sista xxxxxx

Live the Life
A Soul Survivor Guide to Doing It

Mike Pilavachi with Craig Borlase

It's easy enough being Christians in church or at Christian events, but how do we even begin to live the life when we're back home, at college or at work?

Live the Life helps us get to grips with the key issues that challenge us all:

- how do we deal with temptation and guilt?
- can we hear God speak?
- how can we share our faith?
- what happens when we worship?
- how can we find God in our weakness and failure?
- can prayer be part of our lifestyle?
- how do we know what to do with our lives?

Published by Hodder & Stoughton
ISBN 0 340 71385 2

Soul Survivor Presents: Upwardly Mobile
How to Live a Life of Significance

David Westlake

The glossy mags will give you all the advice you need for a fast-track route to flash cars, crisp suits and a seat on the board. But God's blueprint for life has rather different goals: feeding the hungry, sheltering the poor and loosening the chains of injustice.

It's not quite as difficult as it first sounds. You don't need money, power or fame to become a person of significance in God's eyes. *Upwardly Mobile* will help you discover your potential to make a real difference in the world in which we live.

David Westlake is Youth Director of Tearfund.

Published by Hodder & Stoughton
ISBN 0 340 75654 3